Benedict Weerasena
Carmelo Ferlito

ASSESSING AND ADDRESSING URBAN POVERTY IN MALAYSIA

✦ ✧ ✦

*Social Mobility through
Entrepreneurship*

Monolateral

Assessing and Addressing Urban Poverty in Malaysia: Social Mobility through Entrepreneurship

ISBN: 978-1-946374-28-8

First edition: 1 September 2022

Cover: A Kuala Lumpur slum (Juha Sompinmaeki/Shutterstock)

Typeset in Minion 3 and Museo Sans, cover in Bebas Neue Pro.

Monolateral
Richardson, Texas (USA)
monolateral.com
editor@monolateral.com

CONTENTS

Part I

Part II

Foreword

THE SUSTAINABLE DEVELOPMENT GOALS (SDGs), set up in 2015 by the United Nations and adopted by all member states, have provided truly worthwhile aims for Malaysia and the world to aspire to by 2030.

A key principle behind the SDGs is "leaving no one behind", which encapsulates its inclusiveness.

In the cities, the pandemic years have seen many of those in the Bottom 40 per cent group lose their means of income as a lot of jobs cannot be carried out from the confines of home, the on-going pandemic questioning the adequacy of the country's safety nets are not adequate.

Besides that, the urban poor face the obstacle of both unaffordable and low quality housing. People's Housing Project flats continue to experience issues with cleanliness, drainage and wiring, leaving many flats dilapidated. Add to that the worry of waste management that continues to plague urban Malaysia.

Sadly, less than 30 per cent of the country's waste is separated and recycled, with the rest going to landfills, resulting in the release of toxins to surrounding areas.

The above are just a few of the significant problems encountered throughout the country in attaining the SDGs. To overcome this, two very important principles have to be adopted. Firstly, solutions need to be bottom-up as opposed to top-down.

The communities themselves understand their problems the best and should be allowed to provide solutions. Diktats from higher authorities imposed on every locality will not always be helpful in supporting the poorest communities.

Secondly, solutions must also empower communities. Under the All-Parliamentary Party Group, many projects have been carried out, such as micro-entrepreneurship training for the B40, etc. These projects help provide many with the skills and abilities to be able to help themselves.

2030 is less than a decade away. There is certainly much progress that Malaysia has made in recent years that the country should be proud of, but if the principle of "leaving no one behind" is to become a reality, SDGs have to start being more relevant for everyone.

Tackling urban poverty in Malaysia requires the right set of tools, as there is no single magic solution to resolve urban poverty. This set of tools can be divided into three components: shelter, financial assistance and employment. Each component requires short-term solutions and long-term investment to reorganise and repurpose existing infrastructure and society.

Importantly, implementing these solutions calls for the right coalition of actors, not only focusing on poverty as a political or racial issue but addressing it as a constant socio-economic problem besetting the whole country.

While the world is becoming a much more urban place – and the future of Humanity is undoubtedly urban – as Ambassador of the Kingdom of Belgium in Malaysia, I am honoured and grateful to have humbly helped trigger launching a study and a report to pave the way for bold and concrete actions to address the pervasive presence of urban poverty and inequality in our societies.

Pascal H. GRÉGOIRE
July 2022

Executive Summary

THE PRESENT PAPER aims to assess and address urban poverty in Malaysia. While we rely on previous research for data, we believe that our critical assessment of the issue and the proposed way to address it are original, offering a relevant contribution to the policy debate for further action both at the legislative level and on the ground.

Part I: Assessing urban poverty.

- As Malaysia emerges from the COVID-19 pandemic, decades of progress in successful poverty reduction have been reversed, especially in urban areas nationwide. The lockdown measures have resulted in rising unemployment and underemployment, decreased salaries, and reduced household incomes, which contributed to elevated levels of poverty.
- In comparison with the rural poor, the urban poor bore the brunt of the pandemic due to widespread commerce closures that impacted informal business activity in cities, the inability to transition to remote working arrangements, a substantial reduction of salaries and wages, elevated urban food insecurity, and cramped quarters in low-cost housing projects.
- The number of hardcore poor households in Kuala

Lumpur rose exponentially by 269 per cent from 1,048 in 2019 to 3,865 in 2021. Similarly, both Putrajaya and Labuan recorded a multifold increase in hardcore poor households in 2021.

- The urban poor of Kuala Lumpur faced many challenges during the pandemic, including financial difficulties and depleted savings, higher risk of malnutrition, stunting and wasting, the absence of social safety nets, and limited educational accessibility among the young.

- In terms of addressing urban poverty gaps, the current measurement method needs to be updated and improved to address several statistical issues, including undercounting, exclusion of pockets of poverty, and practical issues such as inclusion and exclusion error.

- Pockets of vulnerable urban groups that are in danger of falling through the cracks include the self-employed, own-account and informal workers, the urban elderly population, and non-Malaysian citizens, such as documented and undocumented migrant workers, stateless communities, refugees and asylum seekers.

- The inadequate coverage of social protection schemes – especially social insurance mechanisms and active labour market policies – threatens to trap many more households in poverty in the event of an economic shock.

- Although access to microfinancing schemes abound in Malaysia, the coverage, efficiency and effectiveness in promoting social mobility leaves much room for improvement.

Part II: Addressing urban poverty.

- The approach embraced in the current work is to move away from the idea of *providing* the urban poor with the resources they do not have, but to *promote* reforms that can place them in the conditions *to earn* the resources they believe they need. Our motto is: ***social mobility through entrepreneurship.***

- While entrepreneurship is recognized as an important driver for social mobility, it does not fall off a tree. Some general reforms are necessary to spur an environment conducive to the development of entrepreneurship among the urban poor:
  - Education reform:
    - Entrepreneurship rests on critical thinking, on the idea of challenging the current way of doing things; for such critical thinking to emerge, we need to recognize a larger role for humanistic disciplines within the pre-university education path.
    - Secondary education should instead develop greater professionalism in order to rebalance expectations and help students in discovering their vocation.
  - To emerge, entrepreneurship requires institutions that promote and protect human liberties; the respect of property rights and the rule of law are the key elements. What emerged from the International Property Rights Index is that Malaysia needs to progress in the fight against corruption and towards political stability.
- These measures, by spurring entrepreneurship, will help the system in moving toward a different growth model that is centred on savings and investments rather than on consumption and government spending, which lead instead to household debt and inflation.
- Beyond the long-term effort for entrepreneurship to emerge, thanks to better education and institutional reforms, other practical reforms can be implemented in the short and medium run:

- Housing policy:
  - Rather than providing homes for the poor, the government should focus on rent support schemes for moving away the poor from "ghettos" toward areas where better job opportunities are available.
- Tax reform centred on:
  - Reduced income taxes to free entrepreneurial spirits.
  - A reformed Good and Service Tax, aiming at nudging in favour of saving.
  - An anti-cyclical progressive capital gain tax.
  - Percentage tax designation institutions to support bottom-up welfare initiatives.
- Liberalization of the labour market:
  - A wider ASEAN job market would support Malaysian talents, offer better opportunities internationally, and stimulate competition domestically.
- Improving access to credit:
  - Microbusinesses should be supported as they emerge from the shadow economy: this is the first step for them to have access to credit, and it should be done with specific fiscal schemes for microbusinesses.
  - The credit market can benefit from an increase in the number of financial operators, similar to what happened with the introduction of digital banking licences. More competition can favour the creation of entrepreneurship support initiatives.
  - Healthy government guarantee schemes, supported by fees, can also be a good vehicle, as they are less distortionary than direct government banking.

General Introduction

ALAYSIA'S ONGOING QUADRUPLE quandary of health, economic, political and flood crises have reversed decades of progress in overcoming poverty, especially in urban areas across Malaysia. In the past 2 years, the pandemic, in addition to the prolonged movement curbs, has disproportionately impacted the most vulnerable living in cities. These include informal workers with unstable sources of income, those with the lowest paying jobs and fewest financial buffers, and households in high-density areas, which increases the risk of infections.

Historically, since the introduction of the New Economic Policy 1971-1990 (NEP), Malaysia has demonstrated strong efforts in the fight against poverty, especially in rural areas, as the incidence was generally higher than its urban counterpart. Unfortunately, this had pushed the issue of urban poverty to take a back seat, reversing the trend in recent years.

With the rapid rates of urbanization in recent years and the unprecedented presence of the Covid-19 pandemic, the numbers of the urban poor in the country has swelled. In November 2021, Malaysia's Economic Affairs Minister revealed that urban poverty is 45 per cent higher than rural poverty in the country, highlighting that there are more poor people in the cities than in rural areas (Kaur and Amrie, 2021).

In the midst of the COVID-19 crisis lies a great opportunity to re-evaluate, rethink and reform Malaysia's urban poverty alleviation initiatives. Granted, we have had measured success in reducing absolute poverty in the past few decades, but is this success due to favourable statistical measurements of poverty? Have our national resources been used optimally and effectively to target the hardcore poor without leakages? Have we unintentionally created a generation of dependents on government assistance with no clear graduation policy? How many more individuals, families and communities have fallen through the cracks? Despite the many statistical shortcomings, it is still important to evaluate the current dire state of urban poverty based on available statistics as a starting point towards proposing holistic policy recommendations.

The current study aims at reassessing urban poverty in Malaysia in light of existing data. Furthermore, we will propose a general framework for addressing the issue by introducing a different paradigm: rather than pushing for the eradication of poverty, we will suggest measures to spur social mobility through entrepreneurship, with both short and long run reform suggestions.

Part I

Assessing Urban Poverty

Introduction: A Historical Overview of Urban Poverty up to the Year 2019

P RIOR TO MALAYSIA'S INDEPENDENCE, over half of the households were living in poverty. Malaysia continued to face high poverty incidence in both rural and ur- ban areas, with the overall incidence of poverty in 1970 being 49.3 per cent, despite high economic growth rates during the 1960s. Specifically, the incidence of poverty in rural areas was higher at 58.7 per cent as compared to urban areas at 21.3 per cent, as seen in Figure I.1 (DOSM, 2019).

Hoping to address the high poverty rates in both urban and rural regions, the Malaysian government formulated a range of policies and plans to guide the management of na- tional development during 1970–2000. For instance, long- term core national policies included the New Economic Policy (NEP) 1970–1990 and the National Development Policy (NDP), 1991–2000. Based on a principle of econom- ic growth with equitable distribution, these two national policies aimed for national unity as the goal of development with a two-pronged strategy to achieve it, namely eradicat- ing poverty and restructuring society.

Vision 2020 complemented these core policies; formu- lated in 1991 under the UN's 8th strategic challenge, its pur- pose was to ensure an economically just society in which there is a fair and equitable distribution of the nation's wealth. In addition, a special document titled the National Economic Recovery Plan was formulated after the 1997 Asian Financial Crisis to strengthen economic fundamentals and continue the equitable socio-economic agenda. Among other plans, which indirectly uplifted many Malaysians from poverty through the development of new industries and better income-generating job opportunities, were the Industrial Masterplans, National Agriculture Policies, and the Privatization Master Plan (EPU, 2020). Summarizing, the plans above, in addition to targeted poverty eradication measures in Malaysia, incorporated eight critical strategies, namely:

1. Agreeing on the definition and measurement of poverty;
2. Increasing productivity and diversifying sources of income;
3. Targeting the hardcore poor through a special program focused on their needs and delivering other appropriate assistance to improve their situations;
4. Involving the private sector and nongovernmental organizations;
5. Improving the quality of life of the poor by providing infrastructural and social amenities, such as piped water, electricity, roads, medical and health services, and schools for the rural population;
6. Providing welfare assistance directed at the poor who were aged or disabled and therefore not employable;
7. Maintaining stable prices, a strategy that involved government intervention in the markets of a small number of food and other essential items; and
8. Reducing or eliminating income tax rates for the poor (EPU, 2004).

The strategies outlined above did bear fruit, as absolute poverty[1] rates declined substantially, especially in rural areas, as seen in Figure I.1. Remarkably, Malaysia's success in poverty alleviation was acknowledged globally, and the relatively young democracy was considered among the fastest countries to achieve the first goal of the Millennium Development Goals (MDG), that of halving poverty by 2010 (EPU, 2020).

That being said, there were still numerous shortcomings in anti-poverty strategies, such as inefficient implementation plagued with mismanagement, waste, abuse of incumbency and leakage of funds; a top-down bureaucratic approach that lead to a culture of dependency; inter-agency duplication and the lack of coordination, leading to inclusion and exclusion errors, among others (Lim, Chander and Hunter, 2021).

More significantly, the successful substantial drop in absolute poverty rates from 1970 to 2016 is, in reality, inaccurate; an unduly low poverty line is used that does not reflect the real cost of living and excludes vulnerable populations from official figures (The Star, 2019). In other words, flaws in statistical measurement of the Poverty Line Income (PLI) result in vast undercounting of poverty rates, masking the dire need for additional efforts.

As evidence, several other research projects and surveys conducted before the pandemic hit highlight a much more acute situation in which many vulnerable urban households are still struggling to make ends meet, especially due to the higher cost of living. For example, households with monthly

---

1 Absolute poverty is defined as insufficient household income to meet the basic needs of food, shelter and clothing, or households in which income is below the Poverty Line Income (PLI). The Department of Statistics Malaysia (DOSM) calculates the PLI using the Cost of Basic Needs approach, which in essence means that the PLI is derived based on Food PLI, based on nutritional needs, and Non-food PLI, based on consumption patterns and necessities of low-income households.

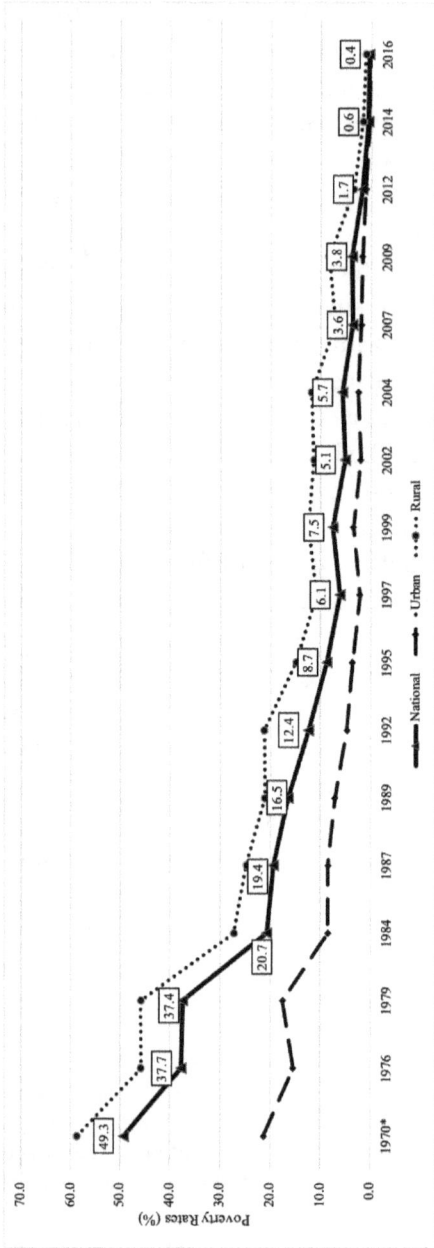

Figure I.1 Absolute Poverty rates declining since 1970. Source: DOSM (2019).

incomes under RM5,000 were forced to reduce their food consumption between 2014 and 2016 (KRI, 2018), despite spending more money for it.

Besides that, around half of Kuala Lumpur's PPR flat[2] low-income households were unable to afford sufficient food from time to time, according to a UNICEF study (UNICEF, 2018). Worryingly, 1 in 3 Malaysians can only cover at most a week's worth of expenses if they lose their income source, while 3 in 4 Malaysians find it an uphill task to raise RM1,000 of immediate cash money for emergencies (BNM, 2016).

To better reflect current needs that emphasize optimal food intake and quality non-food basic requirements, the PLI was revised from RM980 to RM2,208, based on the basic requirements for a household to live healthily and actively (DOSM, 2019). As a result of this upward revision, the absolute poverty rate of 0.4 per cent in 2016 (Figure I.1) was revised to 7.6 per cent. From this realistic value in 2016, the incidence of absolute poverty improved to 5.6 per cent in 2019. Similarly, the incidence of absolute poverty in urban and rural areas also recorded a decrease to 3.8 percent and 12.4 percent respectively, as shown in Figure I.2. Meanwhile, hardcore poverty[3] improved to 0.4 percent in 2019 as compared to 0.6 per cent in 2016.

I.1. The Impact of COVID-19 Pandemic on Employment, Income and Poverty

Beyond just a global health crisis, the COVID-19 pandemic

2 People Housing Project (PPR) is an initiative by the Malaysian government to provide low-cost housing for households that qualify, meeting the housing needs of the low-income group (B40) with a monthly income of RM2,500 or less.

3 Hardcore poverty is defined as households with a monthly household income less than the food Poverty Line Income (PLI).

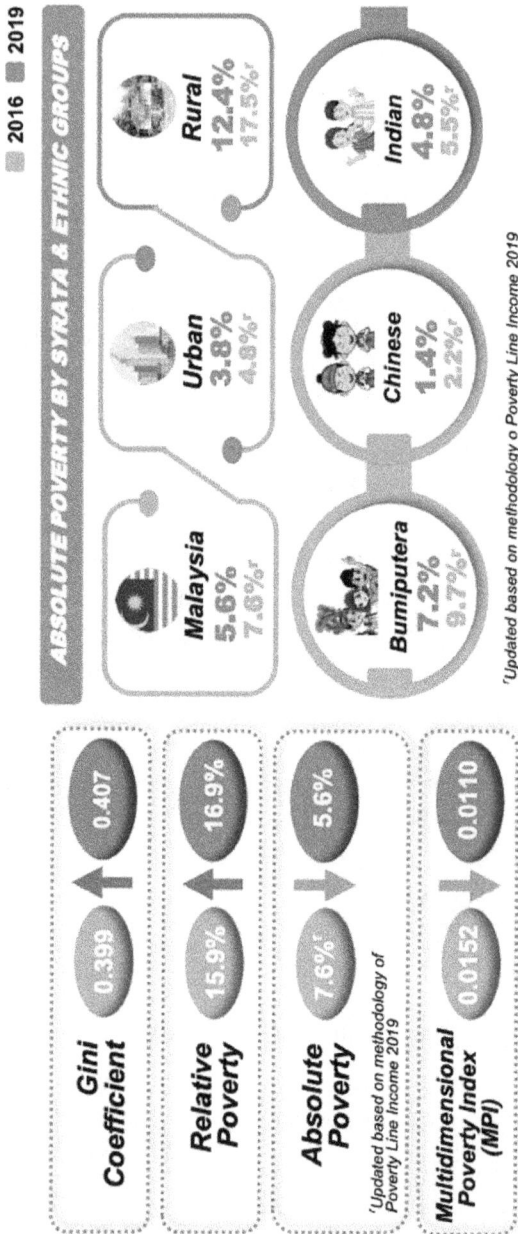

Figure I.2: Both Urban and Rural Absolute Poverty decreased in 2019. Source: DOSM (2019).

was also a social and economic crisis. As many economic sectors came to a standstill with prolonged lockdown measures, unemployment and underemployment increased as salaries plunged. The implementation of the first Movement Control Order (MCO) on 18 March 2020 and subsequent MCOs, as seen in Figure I.3, have caused many economic sectors – especially non-essentials – to temporarily close their businesses, with severe repercussions in the long term.

Many sectors of the economy literally came to a standstill; as a result unemployment and underemployment increased, especially among the lower and middle-income households. For instance, Malaysia's unemployment rate rose to a peak of 5.3 per cent in May 2020 from 3.3 per cent in February 2020. The overall annual rate was 4.5 per cent in 2020 and 4.6 per cent in 2021, which registered the highest rates since 1993 (4.1 per cent) (DOSM, 2021b). Unemployment has remained elevated, with the latest data recording 4.2 per cent as of January 2022, as seen in Figure I.4 (DOSM, 2022).

In 2020, skill-related underemployment[4] increased by 18.9 per cent, or an additional 288,900 persons, to a total of 1.8 million employed persons (38 per cent of total employed) working in lower-skilled jobs than their academic qualifications. On the other hand, the rate of time-related underemployment[5] increased to 2.2 per cent (2019: 1.3 per cent), to record a total of 334,000 employed persons, with an addition of 142,000 employed persons experiencing time-related underemployment as a result of the pandemic (DOSM, 2021b).

---

4 Those with tertiary education and working in the semi-skilled and low-skilled category.

5 Those who are employed less than 30 hours during the reference week because of the nature of their work or due to insufficient work and are able and willing to accept additional hours of work.

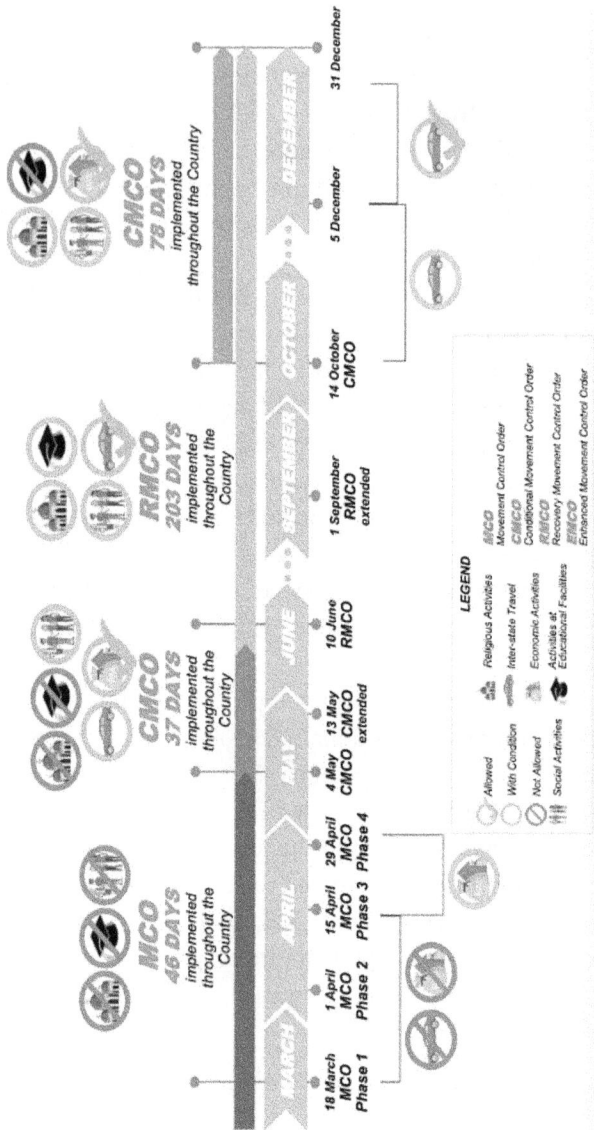

Figure I.3: Timeline of the implementation of Movement Control Order (MCO) in 2020. Source: DOSM (2021a).

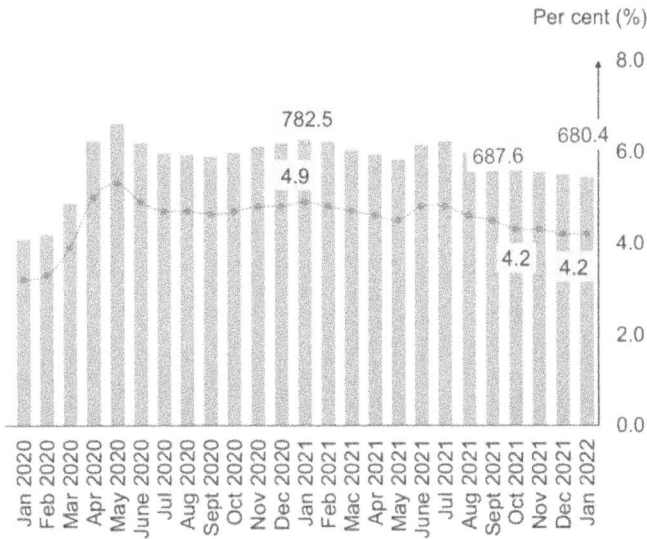

Figure I.4: Unemployed persons and unemployment rate rose and remained elevated up until January 2022.
Source: DOSM (2022).

Besides that, a majority of employees were unable to work remotely or online when business operations could not be conducted as usual, as the largest segment of employed persons in Malaysia was in the semi-skilled category. Consequently, in terms of salaries and wages, some businesses opted to offer reduced wages or unpaid leave to their employees. Based on the *Salaries and Wages Survey Report 2020*, the average salaries and wages shrunk by 9.0 per cent from RM3,224 in 2019 to RM2,933 in 2020. The median salary and wages fell a larger 15.6 per cent from RM2,442 to RM2,062, as shown in Figure I.5 (DOSM, 2021c).

In terms of household income, the median and mean monthly household gross income recorded a substantial decrease of 11.3 per cent and 10.3 per cent respectively from 2019 to 2020. In absolute values, the mean fell from

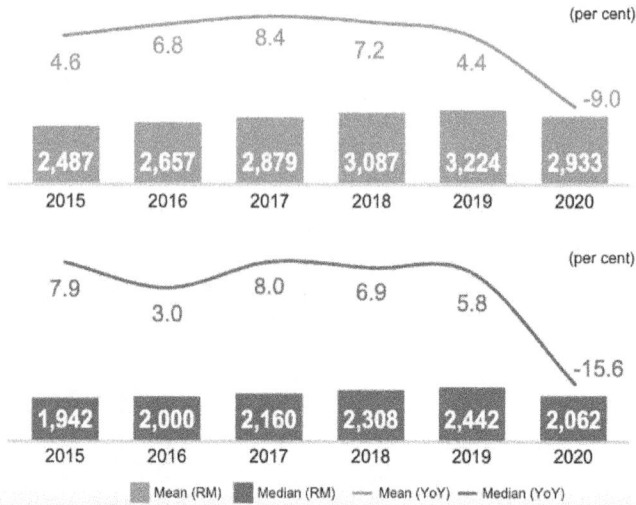

Figure I.5: Mean and median salaries fell drastically in 2020.
Source: DOSM (2021c).

RM7,901 in 2019 to RM 7,089 in 2020, while the median fell from RM5,873 to RM5,209 (DOSM, 2021a). If we break down this decrease in terms of sources of income, paid employment and self-employment – which were the main sources of income – recorded a drop of 16.1 per cent and 9.7 per cent respectively, as shown in Figure I.6. Households or individuals who experienced loss or reduction of income, besides the reduction of working hours and the increase in skill-related underemployment, contributed to this notable decline. On the contrary, current transfers received rose by 14.4 per cent due to numerous government stimulus packages and other assistance that helped ease the financial burden of the household (DOSM, 2021a).

As seen in Figure I.6, the percentage contribution of paid employment to total household income fell from 61.6 per cent to 57.7 per cent, while the contribution of transfers increased slightly from 8.2 per cent to 10.4 per cent in

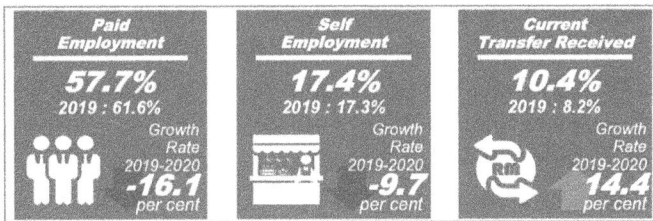

Figure I.6: Income through paid employment and self-employment decreased while current transfers received increased in 2020. Source: DOSM (2021a).

2020 (DOSM, 2021a). This highlights a worrying phenomenon in which Malaysian households became increasingly dependent on current transfers as their source of income during the pandemic. Obviously this form of dependency is unsustainable if it continues in the long term, with the government facing limited fiscal capacity to continuously ease the financial burdens of many households struggling to survive during an economic shock.

All in all, the adverse impacts noted above of rising unemployment and underemployment, decreased salaries, and reduced household incomes all resulted in elevated levels of poverty across Malaysia. This highlights the point that the different types of confinement policies, introduced with the intention of slowing the spread of the virus, indirectly exacerbated existing socio-economic problems and created new ones. As seen across the world, the most affected communities and households have been those who were already most at risk of poverty and exclusion.

According to the latest statistics available[6] from the Department of Statistics Malaysia (2021a), the incidence of

---

6 The latest statistics available from the Department of Statistics Malaysia on household income, poverty rates, salaries and wages are usually published in the third quarter (Q3) of the year for the preceding year. As such, the data for the aspects above for the year 2021 will only be

absolute poverty increased from 5.6 per cent in 2019 to 8.4 per cent in 2020. Hence, the COVID-19 health and economic crisis reversed the progress made on reducing absolute poverty from the higher pre-2016 rate of 7.6 per cent. The 8.4 per cent in 2020 translates into 639,800 households trapped in absolute poverty, in which household income is insufficient to meet the basic needs of food, shelter and clothing; this is a substantial rise from 405,400 households across Malaysia in 2019, as shown in Figure I.7.

In the year of 2020, estimated **639.8 thousand** of households falls under absolute poor household

	Absolute poverty	**Hardcore** poverty	**Relative** poverty
2020	*8.4%*	*1.0%*	*16.2%*
2019	*5.6%*	*0.4%*	*16.9%*

Figure I.7: Absolute poverty and hardcore poverty rose in 2020. Source: DOSM (2021a).

Meanwhile, hardcore poverty is estimated to increase from 0.4 per cent in 2019 to 1.0 per cent in 2020, amounting to 78,000 households whose monthly income is less than half of the poverty line income, or under RM1,104 (DOSM, 2021a). Before the pandemic, a rate of 0.4 per cent implied that Malaysia had virtually eradicated hardcore poverty as a result of previous poverty alleviation programmes, which include additional opportunities to enhance employability and income, better housing, and food and educational assistance for children. Yet, pockets of hardcore poverty still persist in rural and urban areas, with a higher incidence of poverty prevalent among the Orang Asli and other indigenous communities living in remote areas. This issue of hardcore poverty will continue to fester post-pandemic

published in Q3 2022.

if no proactive actions are taken to address those who fall through the cracks.

Meanwhile, relative poverty decreased from 16.9 per cent in 2019 to 16.2 per cent in 2020, accounting for 1.2 million households in relative poverty (DOSM, 2021a). The reason for this slight decrease is a significant drop in overall household income, thus decreasing the median value of income for 2020 compared to 2019[7]. This interesting outcome also implies that the income level of most M40 families has been substantially impacted by the health and economic crisis. As evidence, 20 per cent of households from the M40 group with income between RM4,850 and RM10,959 moved to the B40 group in 2020 (DOSM, 2021a).

Comparing the states across Malaysia, all states recorded an increase in absolute poverty except Federal Territory Putrajaya, as shown in Figure I.8. In 2020, Sabah recorded the highest incidence of absolute poverty (25.3 per cent), followed by Kelantan (21.2 per cent) and Sarawak (12.9 per cent). Meanwhile, the largest increase in absolute poverty was recorded in Kelantan, with a significant increase in poverty by 8.8 percentage points to 21.2 per cent, from 12.4 per cent the year before, followed by Terengganu by 5.9 percentage points to 12.0 per cent, from 6.1 per cent (DOSM, 2021a).

I.2. Current State of Urban Poverty

As the COVID-19 pandemic hit, the adversve socio-economic impact on urban poverty was greater than on rural

---

7 Relative poverty is defined by the Department of Statistics as a situation where average monthly household income is below half of the national median household income. Thus, relative poverty is not measured using the PLI but looks at the living standards determined by household income.

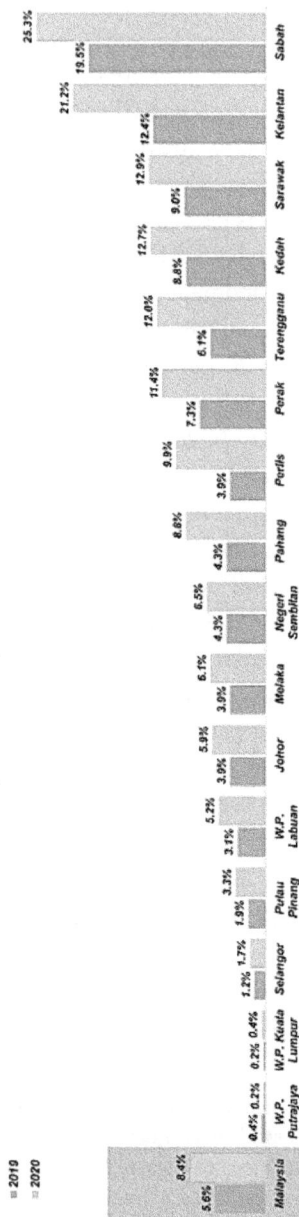

Figure I.8: All states recorded a rise in absolute poverty, except Putrajaya. Source: DOSM (2021a).

poverty for several reasons. First, the more aggressive distancing and containment measures crucial in impacted urban areas resulted in widespread commerce closures, which disproportionately affected the informal business activity on which many lower-income urban households depended. In addition, strict limits on travel led to large declines in urban human mobility, especially on public transit, and particularly in the largest cities. This was also due to epidemiological models that predicted that, without mitigation strategies, the virus would spread faster in urban metropolitan areas than in rural areas (Stier, Berman and Bettencourt, 2020).

Second, a large share of lower-income workers in urban areas who held service jobs in hospitality, childcare, retail and personal services, all of which depend on face-to-face interactions, could not transition towards remote work arrangements. In the first year of the pandemic with no vaccine in sight, the inability to work from home for those types of jobs exacerbated the risk of the virus spreading.

Third, containment measures and supply chain bottlenecks across the globe threatened to worsen food insecurity among urban dwellers. Moreover, transportation and logistical challenges from rural agricultural producers caused an increase in food commodity prices, which further burdened the urban poor.

Next, cramped living spaces, particularly in low-cost high-rise homes such as the urban People's Housing Projects (*Projek Perumahan Rakyat*, or PPR), made quarantine almost impossible. Furthermore, the lack of conducive living conditions impeded access to online learning, in addition to the challenges of the digital divide.

This magnifies the fact that types of employment and housing conditions were key determinants for maintaining income, health and quality of life during the pandemic. With these challenges, in addition to worsened mental health issues due to uncertainties and overcrowding, urban poor were certainly badly hit as a result of the health crisis.

In terms of monthly salaries and wages, urban employees experienced a substantial decrease in the midst of the pandemic. With reference to Figure I.9, the mean monthly salaries and wages in urban areas across Malaysia decreased by 9.3 per cent, or RM316, to RM3,089 in 2020, down from RM3,405 in 2019 (DOSM, 2021c). This reversed the previous positive growth trend from 2015 to 2019. The reasons for the unprecedented decrease include the loss of job opportunities, reduced working hours, or a drop in the nominal wages of workers.

Similarly, median monthly salaries and wages of urban employees declined as compared to the previous year. A double-digit negative growth of 11.6 per cent was recorded in 2020, with urban salaries and wages falling to RM2,268 from RM2,565 in 2019, as shown in Figure I.10 (DOSM, 2021c). One possible explanation for why the decline in median salary and wages was larger than the mean is because the latter is influenced by outliers. Hence, it is most

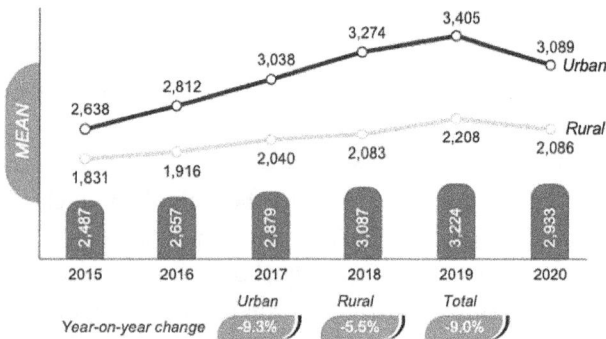

Figure I.9: Mean salaries and wages of urban employees fell 9.3 per cent in 2020. Source: DOSM (2021c).

likely that salaries in the top income bracket (as an outlier) kept the mean salary higher than the fall in median salary.

As a result of decreasing salaries and wages, overall household income has fallen, resulting in more households being pushed into lower-income groups. As evi-

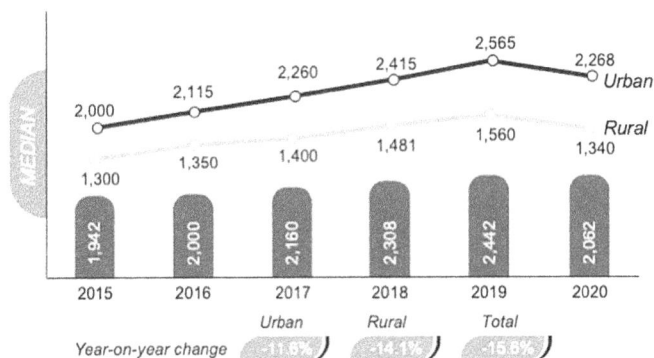

Figure I.10: Median salaries and wages of urban employees fell 11.6 per cent in 2020. Source: DOSM (2021c).

dence, around 580,000 households that were previously in the M40 category slipped into the B40 classification due to the effects of the pandemic on the nation's economy. This accounts for an estimated 20 per cent of M40 households (DOSM, 2021a).

In terms of the latest data on urban poverty, the Department of Statistics Malaysia did not publish poverty data according to strata for the year 2020[8]. However, several other sources of data reveal the severe impact of the health and economic crisis on the urban poor. For instance, data from the Ministry of Federal Territories revealed that the number

---

8 The household income estimates and incidence of poverty in 2020 were calculated without conducting the Household Income and Basic Amenities Survey (HIS/BA), which is usually conducted twice every five years. Hence, statistics by strata (urban vs rural) and further detailed dimensions are not available for publication by this study.

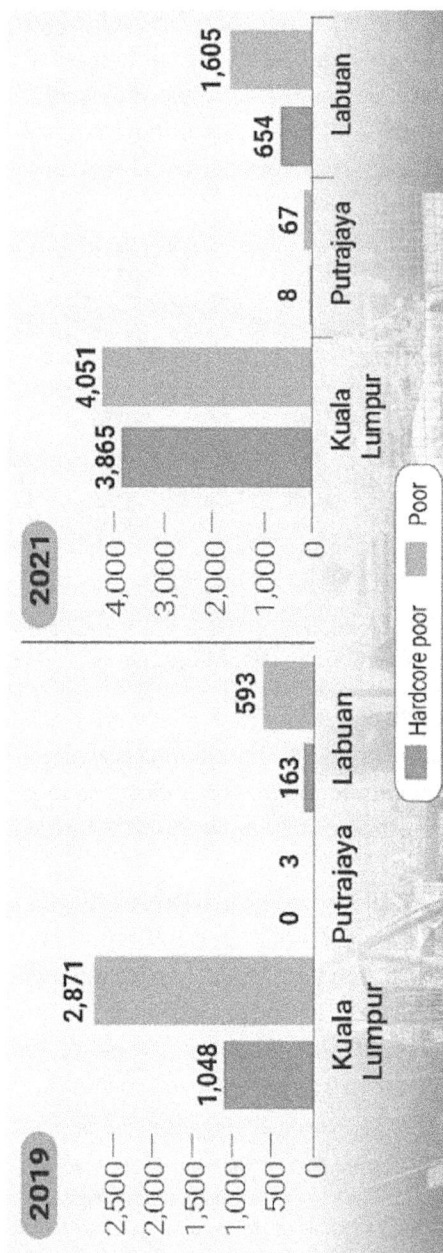

Figure I.11: Exponential rise in hardcore poor and poor households in Malaysia's Federal Territories, 2021. Source: Wahab (2022).

of hardcore poor households in Kuala Lumpur rose exponentially by 269 per cent from 1,048 in 2019 to 3,865 in
2021 (Wahab, 2022). The number of poor households also
increased from 2,871 to 4,051, as shown in Figure I.11. Similarly, there was a multifold increase in both Putrajaya and
Labuan, in which 8 and 654 hardcore poor households were
recorded in 2021.

It is important to highlight that these statistics on poverty and on hardcore poverty depend on the poverty line
income (PLI), which is derived based on Food PLI, comprised of nutritional needs, and on Non-food PLI, based on
consumption patterns and necessities of low-income households. Hence when the poverty line is next revised in 2023,
the number of poor and hardcore poor in these Federal Territories and across Malaysia are expected to rise again.

I.3. Analysis of Urban Poverty: A Case Study of Kuala Lumpur's Low-Cost Flats

During the COVID-19 pandemic, UNICEF and UNFPA
jointly commissioned the Families on the Edge study to
explore the impact of the health crisis on 500 low-income
urban families with children in Kuala Lumpur (UNICEF,
2020). This study – which sought to collect significant evidence on the impact on household finances, psychosocial
wellbeing and the relevance, adequacy and accessibility of
mitigation programmes, among others – highlights important gaps in current urban poverty alleviation strategies.

As an overview, absolute poverty rates among Kuala
Lumpur's urban low-cost flats peaked in May 2020 during
the first wave of the pandemic, as seen in Figure I.12. As
movement controls eased, accompanied by the gradual re-
opening of economic sectors, in addition to several rounds
of stimulus packages and government aid disbursement,

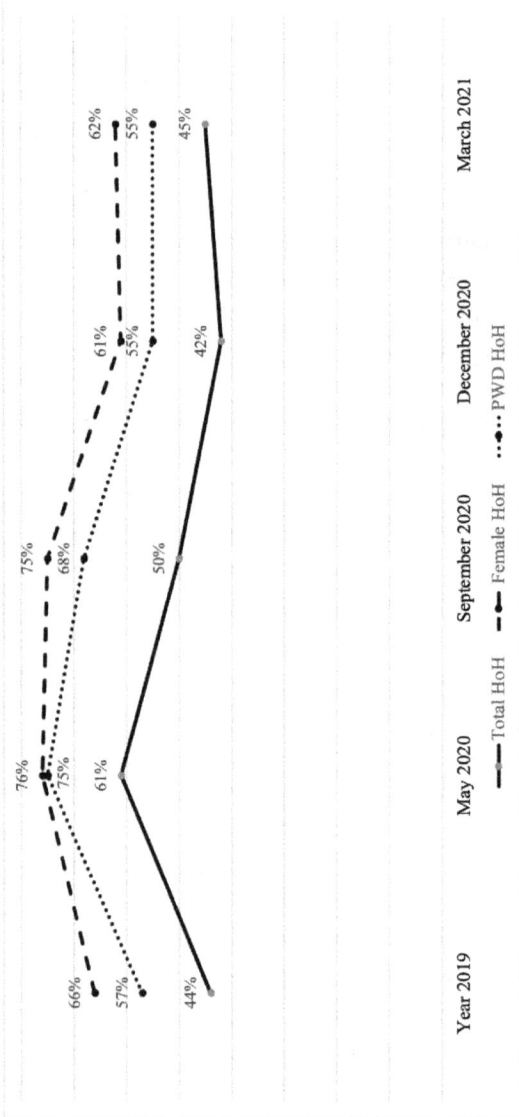

Figure I.12: Absolute poverty rates peaked in May 2020 and tapered down in the following months. Source: UNICEF (2021).

absolute poverty rates tapered downwards, reaching pre-COVID levels as of March 2021.

Referring to Figure I.12, female-headed households experienced higher absolute poverty, followed by households headed by persons with disabilities (PWD), as compared to overall households. This magnifies the exceptional vulnerability faced by female-headed households, to which a myriad of factors contribute, including higher rates of unemployment and lower rates of social protection coverage (UNICEF, 2020). As such, targeted measures and strategies that are tailor-made to these highly vulnerable groups are essential in pursuing equitable development.

To address the rise in absolute poverty, income sources need to be evaluated to better understand the significance of wages and transfers. Referring to Figure I.13, wages still make up a substantial 51 to 75 per cent of the average household income of the urban poor across the demographic breakdown.

Transfers in the form of formal government assistance or informal financial aid from NGOs, friends and family have increased during the pandemic, helping to top up the slight drop in household income from wages and self-employment. Moreover, these transfers helped in the short term to mitigate the socio-economic impact of the crisis, especially in female-headed households and disabled-headed households.

Many respondents gave their feedback, explaining that instead of depending on one-off handouts, more sustainable assistance is much better, such as the assistance of being fully employed. There were also requests for a raise in the amount of aid and for longer-term assistance. In terms of accessibility to assistance, barriers include illiteracy, procedural issues, logistical challenges, and 'cronyism' (UNICEF, 2020).

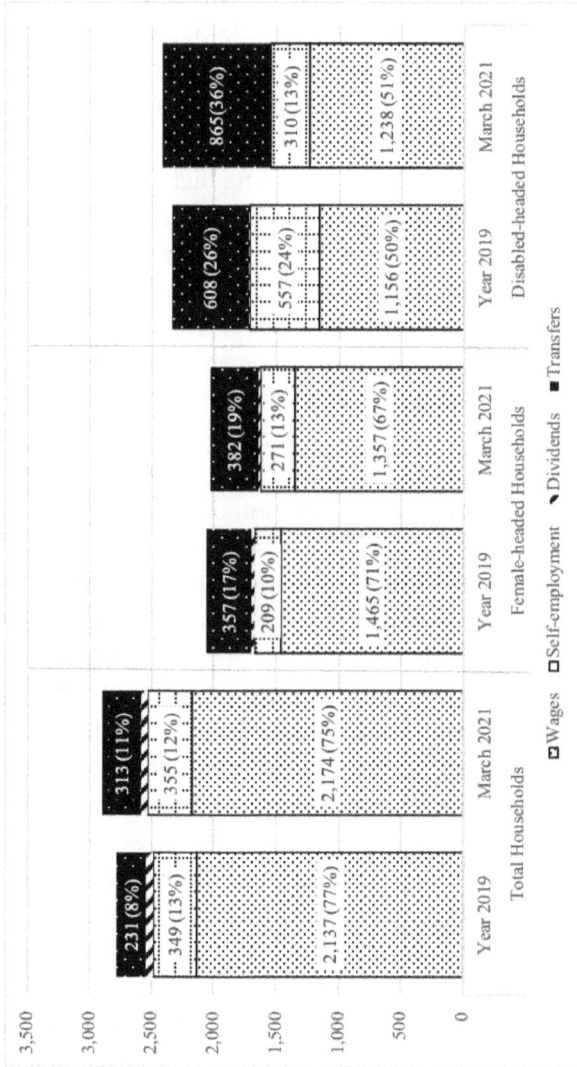

Figure I.13: Transfers are increasingly significant in counterbalancing the loss of personal wages. Source: UNICEF (2021).

In terms of the main coping strategies to deal with financial difficulties, 1 in 3 households and 4 in 10 female-headed households depend on government assistance, with reference to Figure I.14. On the other hand, the most subscribed strategy is to use household savings, in which almost 2 in 5 heads of households (HoH) use their savings to mitigate the reduction of income. With the prolonged crisis threatening to deplete the savings of the urban poor, there is a stronger need to build greater financial resilience against future shocks.

Alarmingly, around a quarter of the respondents choose to reduce their food intake as a coping mechanism when faced with financial difficulties, as shown in Figure I.14. In the long run, this leads to an unhealthy rise in the prevalence of malnutrition, with the risk of stunting and wasting among younger children. This in turn will possibly contribute to greater susceptibility to infectious diseases and irreversible impairment in childhood development among children in urban poor areas. This poverty-nutrition trap induces lifelong socio-economic consequences, including impaired learning potential, compromised future labour productivity, and higher medical expenses, which reinforces a vicious cycle of intergenerational poverty.

Additionally, one major challenge plaguing urban poor households is the absence or partial lack of social protection coverage. Referring to Figure I.15, 45 per cent of heads of households do not have social protection and insurance, as they are not registered with either Employment Provident Fund (EPF) or Social Security Organization (SOCSO). Furthermore, female-headed households are worse off (50 per cent), and households headed by persons with disabilities are the worst off demographic (92 per cent). This leaves many of these households exceptionally vulnerable to ill health, inequality, hardcore poverty and social exclusion

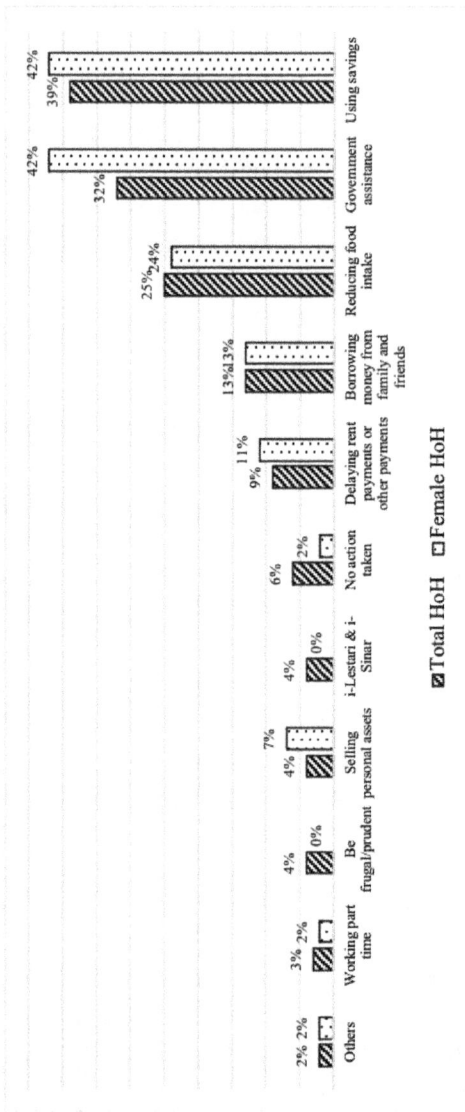

Figure I.14: Main coping strategies to deal with financial difficulties include using savings and government assistance. Source: UNICEF (2021).

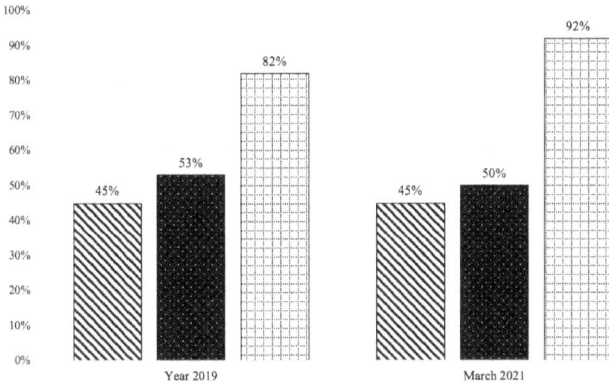

Figure I.15: Lack of social protection among urban poor households. Source: UNICEF (2021).

throughout their lifecycle, which is a significant obstacle to equitable economic and social development.

Moreover, 9 in 10 among the self-employed do not have EPF or SOCSO, indicating the glaring lack of access to employment-based social security and social protection. In other words, these self-employed persons miss out on the crucial comprehensive social security schemes and employment benefits which include the pension fund, basic health and injury insurance, disability benefits, survivors' benefits, and paid annual, sick or maternity leave. This makes them extremely vulnerable when hit by an unexpected circumstance or a national crisis.

School closures certainly have disproportionate impacts on students from vulnerable households, especially in the low-cost flats across Malaysia in which long-term inequality is worsening. Challenges faced among students from lower-income families when they try to study remotely include limited access to technology and connectivity, in addition to the lack of a conducive environment to learn effectively.

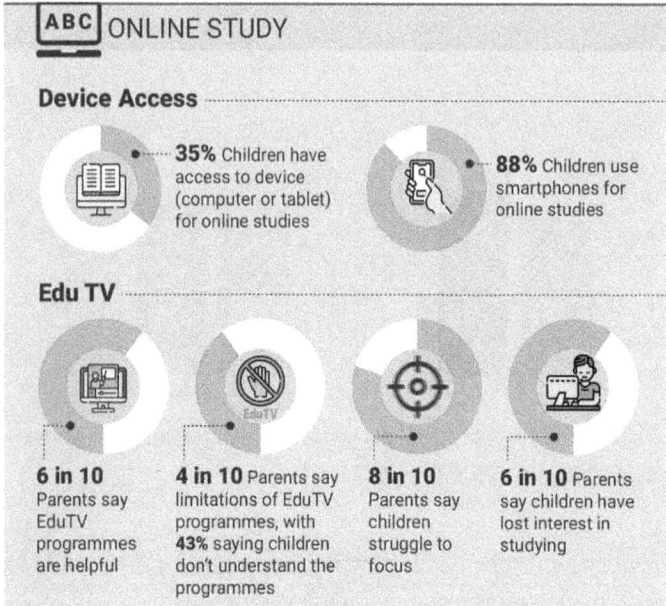

Figure I.16: Educational accessibility and opportunities have been substantially impacted. Source: UNICEF (2021).

As many schools implement distance learning, many underprivileged students missed out due to a lack of devices or the unavailability of their parents' devices during the scheduled lessons (Ong, 2020).

With reference to Figure I.16, 8 out of 10 parents explain that their children struggle to stay focused during online lessons. More worryingly, 60 per cent of the parents surveyed revealed that their children had lost interest in schooling since the movement control order (MCO) was imposed, with 7 per cent of upper secondary students opting not to return to classes (UNICEF, 2020). All in all, these student dropouts are more likely to face challenging future economic hardship, social stigma, fewer job opportunities and lower salaries.

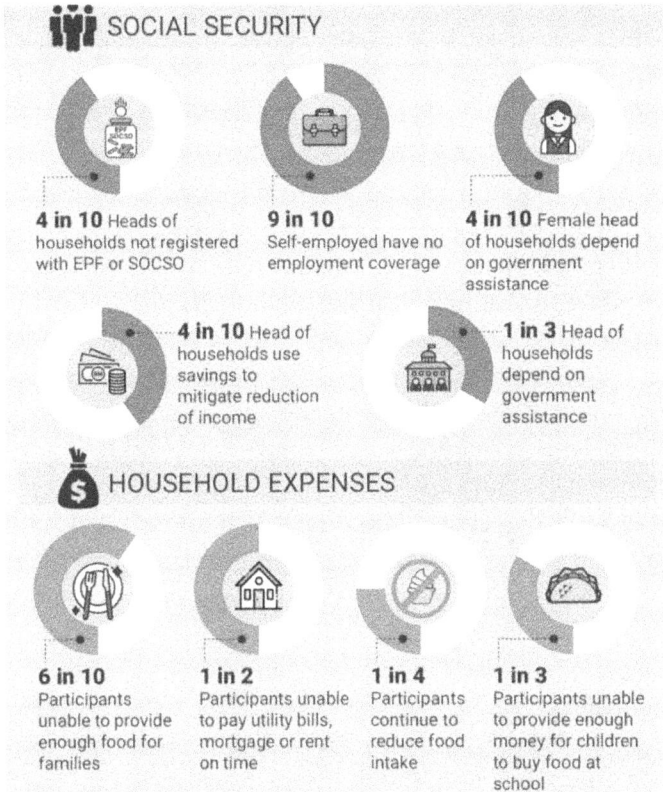

SOCIAL SECURITY

4 in 10 Heads of households not registered with EPF or SOCSO

9 in 10 Self-employed have no employment coverage

4 in 10 Female head of households depend on government assistance

4 in 10 Head of households use savings to mitigate reduction of income

1 in 3 Head of households depend on government assistance

HOUSEHOLD EXPENSES

6 in 10 Participants unable to provide enough food for families

1 in 2 Participants unable to pay utility bills, mortgage or rent on time

1 in 4 Participants continue to reduce food intake

1 in 3 Participants unable to provide enough money for children to buy food at school

Figure I.17: Summary of main issues in Kuala Lumpur's low-cost flats. Source: UNICEF (2021).

I.4. Analysis of Gaps in Urban Poverty

In this section, the gaps which continue to perpetuate urban poverty will be identified, explored and analysed. This is significant to research holistic approaches and new strategies to address and alleviate the plight of urban poor households, to ensure no one is left behind.

I.4.1. Measurement of urban poverty

First of all, poverty needs to be accurately and precisely measured, using the most up-to-date statistics and the right methodology to address technical issues. Otherwise, the measurement of urban poverty will be marred by under-counting, exclusion of pockets of poverty – including the outliers who make up the bottom 10 per cent – and practical issues such as inclusion and exclusion error.

As such, the right approach to measurement is crucial to show a realistic scenario faced by the nation and the right implementation of intervention strategies needed. As evidence, when the poverty line income (PLI) was revised in 2019 from RM980 to RM2,208 to better reflect current needs that emphasize optimal food intake and quality of non-food basic requirements, the earlier illogical absolute poverty rate of 0.4 per cent in 2016 was revised to 7.6 per cent.

Historically the PLI, which was initially designed for five household members, was first introduced in 1977 to calculate extreme poverty. This initial PLI, comprised of the food PLI[9] and the non-food PLI,[10] was calculated at RM252.36 at the start and updated yearly by using the Consumer Price Index (CPI) as a proxy to reflect the changes in prices (Zain, 2007).

In 2005, a revision of the PLI methodology was carried out, using a more comprehensive, inclusive, and detailed calculation approach based on household size, composition, and location (state and stratum). For instance, different food energy requirements for each household, considering

9 A food basket containing selected items totalling 9,910 kcal, as the minimum energy intake of an individual.

10 Clothes, footwear, rent, furniture and household equipment, fuel and power, medical care and health expenses, transport and communication, recreation, education, and cultural services.

its size and composition, were calculated, in which daily kilocalories (kcal) levels were converted to monthly kcal, which are then multiplied by the price per kcal. The national food PLI then was RM620 (EPU, 2021).

Similarly, the calculation of non-food PLI, which incorporated Ravallion's approach (1998) to capture the low-income household spending trend on non-food items, was more comprehensive than the previous mechanism. Specifically, five types of non-food PLI were determined, such as clothing, durables, housing, transport and other non-food items, that overall included 106 items. The national PLI in 2005 was RM690 (Ravallion, 1998). Every five years, the PLI will be revised twice based on this methodology, taking into account changes in price and consumption. After several upward revisions, the national PLI for 2016 was at RM980.

In 2019, the PLI methodology was revised again, with the food PLI component designed based on optimum minimum daily food intake using a healthy and nutritious food-based dietary guidelines approach, instead of merely considering subsistence (EPU, 2021). This optimum minimum concept refers to the optimum nutrients requirement based on the 2020 Malaysian Dietary Guidelines (MDG) and 2017 Recommended Nutrient Intakes for Malaysia (RNI). Using this approach, the national food PLI was RM1,169 per month with an average national household size of 3.9 (DOSM, 2019). On the other hand, the non-food PLI was revised to RM1,038 per month, considering not only the minimum quantity (146 items) but the quality of spending as well. This totalled up to a national PLI of RM2,208, which increased from RM980 in 2016.

Yet, the new Poverty Line Income (PLI) of RM2,208 as of 2019 is still considered low and needs to be revised upwards. This is in accordance with the post-pandemic era of rising prices of both food and non-food items across Malaysia. In addition, this PLI rate is unable to sufficiently address living conditions, especially in the urban areas of Klang Valley, Johor and Penang. To put it in perspective, this latest PLI is still lower than the expected minimum living wage of RM2,700 for a single adult residing in Kuala Lumpur, as proposed by the Bank Negara Malaysia (BNM, 2018). The APPGM-SDG Secretariat and Malaysian CSO-SDG Alliance (2021) propose a strategic approach based on international best practices for an updated revision:

> World Bank classifies Malaysia as an Upper Middle-Income Country and hence, a better measurement of PLI would be USD5.50 a day. Another alternative would be to use 60 per cent of the median income as the PLI as is done in OECD countries, in which case would be RM3,524 a month. The policy implications of using the different PLIs are huge (APPGM-SDG Secretariat and Malaysian CSO-SDG Alliance, 2021, p. 5).

Beyond just the PLI as a measurement of poverty, it is crucial to focus on multidimensional poverty deprivation in addition to the monetary dimension. Hence in 2016, the Government introduced the Multidimensional Poverty Index (MPI) to evaluate poverty from a more inclusive perspective, based on the four dimensions of education, health, standard of living, and income, with a total of eleven indicators.

As seen in Table I.1, household deprivation for almost all indicators has decreased, except for living quarters conditions. For instance, years of schooling (1.2 per cent in 2016 fell to 1.0 per cent deprivation in 2019), access to healthcare facilities (6.8 to 6.5 per cent deprivation), access to clean water (4.1 to 3.9 per cent deprivation), room crowdedness

(12 to 9.5 per cent deprivation), garbage collection facilities (14.9 to 13.3 per cent deprivation), basic communication tools (1.4 to 1.1 per cent deprivation) and monthly gross income (7.6 to 5.6 per cent deprivation). Remarkably, other deprivation indicators are below 1 per cent, such as school attendance (0.4 per cent), toilet facilities (0.4 per cent), and transportation facilities (0.6 per cent) (EPU, 2021).

However, there is also a need to review the mechanisms used to measure the multi-dimensional poverty index (MPI) as the indicators and targets used are set at very low thresholds and are not realistic (APPGM-SDG Secretariat and Malaysian CSO-SDG Alliance, 2021).

I.4.2. Social exclusion of pockets of vulnerable groups

In the age of fast-growing metropolitan cities and rapid urban growth, pockets of vulnerable groups are still being locked out of the benefits of development. These groups fall through the cracks and gaps of urban modernization and human capital development, and they potentially miss out on poverty alleviation programmes. Termed 'Social Exclusion', these groups are deprived of the choices and opportunities to escape from poverty, with some trapped for multiple generations.

First, there is a need to ensure poverty alleviation programmes reach the 2.8 million affected B40 households, with no one left behind. A large number of these groups who live in urban areas are casual and low-skilled workers, many of whom work in informal sectors and are more likely to lose their jobs in a crisis, resulting in financial hardship. In addition, these households often struggle with socio-economic challenges including illiteracy, malnutrition and chronic diseases.

Di-mension	Indicators	Deprived if	Incidence of Household Deprivation (%)	
			2016	2019
Education	Schooling Years	All household members aged between 13 to 60 years have less than 6 years of education	1.2	1.0
	School Attendance	Any children aged between 6 to 12 years are not schooling	0.4	0.4
Health	Access to Health Services	Distance to healthcare facility more than 5 km and no mobile health facility	6.8	6.5
	Access to clean water supply	Other than treated pipe water inside house and water pipe/standpipe	4.1	3.9
Living Standards	Living quarters conditions	Dilapidated or deteriorating	2.9	3.7
	Crowd-edness	More than 2 household members in a bedroom	12.0	9.5
	Home toilet utility	Other than pour or flush toilet	0.3	0.4
	Access to garbage collection	No garbage collection facility	14.9	13.3
	Usage of transportation services	All members in the household do not use private or public transport	0.5	0.6
	Access to basic communication utilities	Does not have consistent fixed line phone or mobile phone	1.4	1.1

Di-mension	Indicators	Deprived if	Incidence of Household Deprivation (%)	
			2016	2019
Income	Mean monthly house-hold gross income	Monthly household gross income less than mean household PLI	7.6	5.6

Table I.1: Multidimensional Poverty Index indicators show improvement. Source: EPU (2021).

Moreover, many of these B40 urban households live in high-density low-cost flats, which puts them at greater risk in the event of a new and more contagious COVID-19 wave. In addition, several of these housing projects are often associated with unfavourable living conditions, domestic violence and abuse, crime and petty theft, as well as drug and alcohol abuse (EPU, 2021). Hence, there is a crucial need to ensure upholding the quality of living and well-being of the urban poor in low-cost flats to improve their social mobility.

For many B40 households, the exclusion rate from government financial aid is quite high. For instance, UNICEF reported that 34 per cent of households with incomes below RM4,000 did not receive 1Malaysia People's Aid (BR1M),[11] despite being qualified (UNICEF, 2018). In addition, as of 2018 only 4 per cent of households living in low-cost flats received Zakat and/or assistance from the social welfare

11 BR1M or *"Bantuan Rakyat 1 Malaysia"* is program is devised under the leadership of Malaysia's 6th Prime Minsiter as part of the government's effort to ease the burden of lower income groups in Malaysia. To be eligible for the "Bantuan Rakyat 1 Malaysia" aid, the recipient's household income must be lower than RM 4000.

department (JKM), as shown in Figure I.18. Hence, many urban poor households fall between the cracks and are excluded from the necessary assistance needed to alleviate poverty.

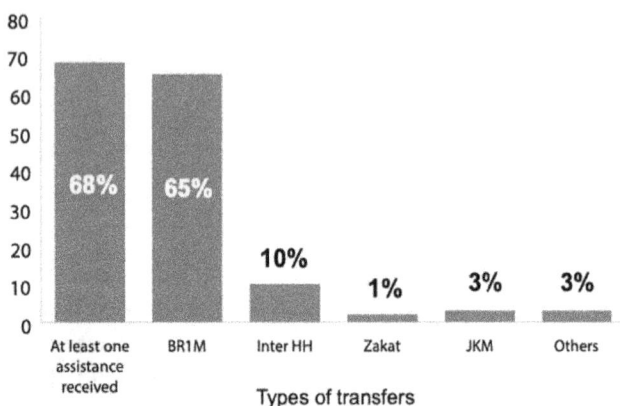

Figure I.18: High exclusion rate from government assistance. Source: UNICEF (2018).

Second, the 2.81 million self-employed, own-account and informal workers make up 19% of the labour force (Lim, 2021). Many of these self-employed and informal workers in urban areas lack the necessary social safety nets as a buffer in the event of an economic shock. A report by the International Labour Organization dramatically illustrates the vulnerability of these workers:

> The defining characteristic of informality – in law or practice not covered by work-related social protection, national labour legislation or entitlement to certain employment benefits (such as paid annual or sick leave) – underscores the vulnerability of these workers. Informal workers often have poor access to healthcare services and have no

income replacement in case of sickness or lockdown. Many have no possibility to work remotely from home. But staying home means losing their jobs, and without income, they starve (Lim, 2021).

The terms of employment put many of these self-employed and informal workers at a disadvantage, including the temporary nature of employment (using fixed-term contracts, including project or task-based contracts, and casual work, including day labour); part-time and on-call work, including zero-hour contracts; multi-party employment engagement (also known as dispatch and labour-hire, which includes temporary agency work and subcontracted labour); and finally disguised employment or dependent self-employment where workers perform services for a business under a civil or commercial contract but depend on one or a few clients for their income and receive direct instructions on how the work is to be carried out (Lim, 2021). During economic crises, those who work in non-standard employment also appear to work shorter hours than standard wage employees, which might result in time-related underemployment. This is often a result of no available extra hours for work instead of a personal decision by choice.

Moreover, the health and economic crisis disproportionately impacted informal workers for two main reasons. First, the sectors in which these urban workers are most represented are also the heaviest hit sectors, including wholesale and retail trade, manufacturing, accommodation and food services (ILO, 2020). Second, a substantial number of these are own-account workers in small businesses of less than ten workers, which are more vulnerable to shocks.

A third potentially excluded group is the urban elderly population who falls through the cracks of urban development. As Malaysia transitioned to an ageing society[12] in 2020 and will age rapidly towards an aged society[13] by 2044, Malaysia will need to address several policy challenges in areas such as employment, income security, health care, and aged care in the coming decades (World Bank, 2020). In urban areas, increases in the cost of living threaten to outstrip retirement savings and incomes, resulting in the risk of vulnerability to future shocks.

EPF recently announced that a substantial 48 per cent of members have less than RM10,000 in their accounts, accounting for the RM101 billion pandemic-related i-Lestari, iSinar and i-Citra withdrawals. Most worryingly, the savings of the bottom 40 per cent of EPF members fell by 38 per cent to just RM8 billion, which amounts to a median savings balance of RM1,005 (Weerasena and Lim, 2022; The Edge Markets, 2021). As a result, the majority of EPF contributors will only receive very low benefits in retirement. Additionally, retirement benefits will be low because participation in covered employment is intermittent and the minimum withdrawal age is low.

Furthermore, EPF coverage is especially low among lower-income households, with less than a fifth of working-age B20 actively contributing to EPF (World Bank, 2020). Alarmingly, almost all old-age income security risks fall on the elderly and their families as a result of the absence of a broad non-contributory social assistance program for older persons. In fact, participation in contributory retirement savings institutions is still low at 60.8 per cent, compared to an aspirational peer group of high-income countries (World Bank, 2020). To put it bluntly, many

---

12 Defined per the international convention as having 7 per cent or more of the population age 65 and above.

13 Defined as having 14 per cent or more of the population age 65 and above.

Malaysians will not be able to retire comfortably over the long term unless concrete mechanisms are put in place to replenish their retirement savings.

Fourth, other excluded pockets of people are urban poor Non-Malaysian citizens, including documented and undocumented migrant workers, stateless communities, refugees and asylum seekers. There are 2 million documented migrant workers (15% of the workforce), in addition to an estimated 2 to 4 million undocumented migrant workers (APPGM-SDG Secretariat and Malaysian CSO-SDG Alliance, 2021); many of these who work in the construction and services industry reside in urban areas. Besides those, there are at least 12,000 stateless people in West Malaysia and possibly tens to hundreds of thousands in Sabah (Lim, 2021).

As of the end of March 2022, there are some 182,120 refugees and asylum-seekers registered with UNHCR in Malaysia. The large majority of 156,110 are from Myanmar, comprising some 103,810 Rohingyas, 22,700 Chins, and 29,600 other ethnic groups from conflict-affected areas or fleeing persecution in Myanmar. The remaining individuals are some 26,000 refugees and asylum-seekers from 50 countries fleeing war and persecution, including some 6,750 Pakistanis, 3,750 Yemenis, 3,320 Syrians, 3,230 Somalis, 2,860 Afghans, 1,640 Sri Lankans, 1,200 Iraqis, 780 Palestinians, and others (UNHCR, 2022).

Many of these non-Malaysian citizens and their families are trapped in urban poverty and live in dire conditions, with some living with poor sanitation and no proper waste management in place. As a result, they face severe risks of waterborne diseases and skin conditions. In addition, many are trapped in generational poverty, as their children – especially stateless children – are unable to access formal education, which is one of the most powerful tools for lifting socially excluded children and adults out of poverty. With limited access to quality education, some stateless children become child labourers, particularly in urban informal workplaces.

All in all, all these pockets of vulnerable communities are socially excluded from reaping the benefits of urbanization and development, with many pushed to the fringes and left far behind in the depths of poverty. Targeted policies for these vulnerable groups are crucial for social mobility in the long term.

I.4.3. The lack of social protection as a safeguard against vulnerabilities

The unprecedented scale and impact of the health and economic crisis have rendered Malaysia's current social protection system insufficient and inadequate in safeguarding the urban poor against vulnerabilities. Indeed, deep structural issues surrounding the current social protection framework have been unearthed. These issues include gaps in overall coverage, fragmented and overlapping programmes, fiscal challenges, and the risk of growing socioeconomic vulnerabilities (BNM, 2020).

Also, many social assistance programmes are founded upon principles of providing a short-term buffer, and they thus lack sustainable financial and legal foundations (KRI, 2021). This leads to unpredictable and less than effective benefits, in addition to under-coverage among urban poor households. Furthermore, the various social assistances programmes introduced deliver benefits rather inefficiently due to the fragmented delivery system.

Referring to Figure I.19, the three core pillars that comprise social protection are protection, prevention, and promotion, which are universally known as the 3Ps. These

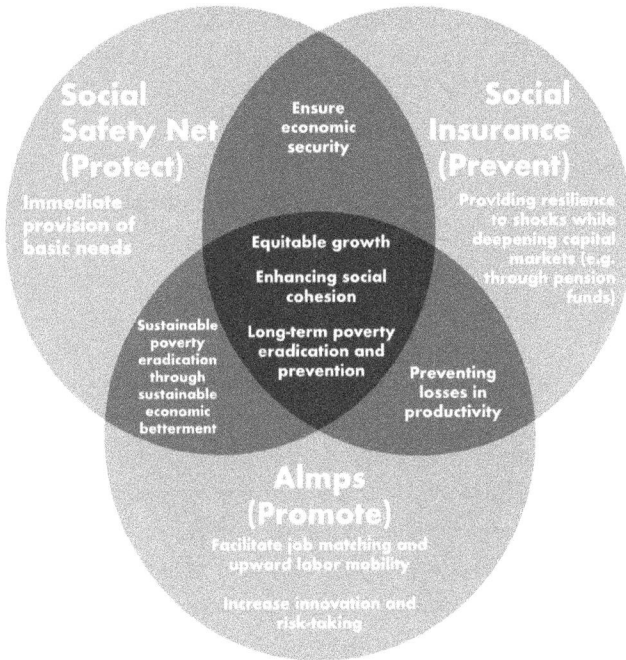

Figure I.19: Malaysia's social protection Measures are overly reliant on social safety nets. Source: BNM (2020).

three main strategies, when collectively executed in an effective and efficient manner, seek to ensure that basic needs are met, resilience against poverty is safeguarded, and economic potential is maximized.

However, Malaysia's social protection system is overly reliant on 'Protect' measures, or on social safety nets such as cash handouts and food baskets. A few reasons for this include that the programmes are short-term stopgap measures that are relatively easier to adopt and implement, as well as being more appealing to the political narrative. A holistic social protection system instead requires placing equal emphasis on longer term social insurance (Prevent) and active labour market policies (ALMP) (Promote).

Hence, the triple crisis centred around the COVID-19 pandemic has presented us with a golden opportunity to plan differently and pursue reforms in social protection measures. We need to build greater resilience through reforming social protection coverage in addition to expanding social insurance and ALMPs to prepare ahead of time for the storms and shocks that may come.

1.4.4. Access to finance

Financial inclusion, and in particular access to financial loans, is key to inclusive growth through the promotion of social mobility among the urban poor. Access to finance opens otherwise blocked advancement opportunities for disadvantaged segments of the population, which is an effective tool to alleviate poverty and address income inequality. This is especially important as a major constraint to starting or doing business is limited access to finance, especially at the micro and small- and medium-sized enterprise (SME) level.

Research has shown that enhanced financial inclusion in developing countries significantly reduces multidimensional poverty, and as a result, improves the lives of the poor (Omar and Inaba, 2020; Salgotra, Kandari and Bahuguna, 2021). In order to maximize society's overall welfare, it is important to promote access to and usage of formal financial services by marginalized segments of the population (Omar and Inaba, 2020). One important foundation for the reduction of poverty here is that overall economic conditions should empower people to use financial access for productive purposes, such as investing in children's education or expanding a business (Park, 2018).

In Malaysia, financial inclusion has been improving steadily over the years, with enhanced efforts to promote

suitable, affordable and quality financial services to all segments of society. This is a result of the Central Bank's drive
towards «an inclusive financial system that best serves all
members of society, including the underserved, to have access to and usage of quality, affordable essential financial
services to satisfy their needs towards shared prosperity»
(BNM, 2017). For instance, Malaysia recorded a higher
financial inclusion index of 0.90 out of 1 in 2015, from an
earlier 0.77 in 2011 (BNM, 2017). However, no updated
data has been published since then.

In terms of overall access to loans, Malaysia has seen a
steady, although minimal, improvement over the years, as
shown in Figure I.20. Overall, Malaysia fares slightly better than its regional and Upper-Middle-Income Country
(UMC) counterparts. However, while other countries dis-
play improvements over the decade, and especially from
2015 to 2016, Malaysia's growth remained relatively stag-
nant. From a score of 1 to 7 (best), Malaysia started off with
a respectable score of 4.55 in 2007, dipped slightly to the
lowest 4.21 in 2010, then slowly picked up the pace over
the next few years to reach a score of 4.71 in 2017. This was
calculated with the latest available data (World Economic
Forum, 2018), showing a year-on-year average growth rate
of 0.42%.

Malaysia also has long-established microfinancing plans
provided by both government agencies and private financial institutions (PFIs). These schemes play an important
role in reducing poverty through supporting the financing
needs of micro enterprises for income generation.

For instance, government initiatives include Amanah
Ikhtiar Malaysia (AIM)[14] as Malaysia's largest microfinance

_____

14 Amanah Ikhtiar Malaysia (AIM) is a private Trust entity incorporated under the Trustee (Incorporation) Act 1952 [Act 258] with the objective of assisting the poor to escape the poverty trap, through providing

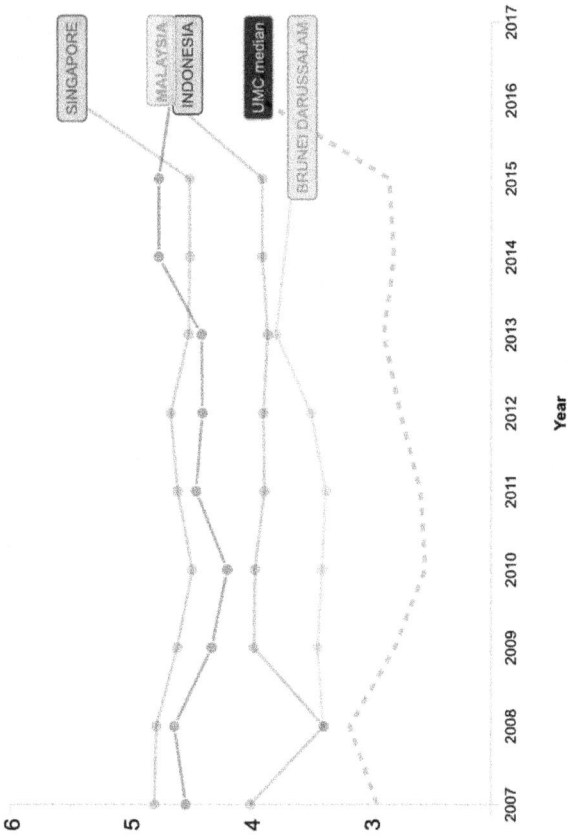

Figure I.20: Malaysia fares slightly better in Ease of Access to Loans than its regional and Upper-Middle-Income Country (UMC) counterparts. Source: World Economic Forum (2018).

institution, which has benefitted over 920,000 borrowers nationwide (Bernama, 2021). In terms of microfinance targeted for the urban poor, AIM offers an urban micro loan that is tailored to poor and low-wage earners living in urban areas. With this loan plan, the hope is that the poor can set up small businesses to increase their income and have a better life in the city (Idris et al, 2021).

It is important to point out that AIM's loans are based on *qard-hasan* (interest-free) principles aligned with Islamic principles of microfinance. However, AIM imposes a 10% service charge, termed *ujrah*, on its loans, which Saad (2012) argued is unusually high due to the unique operation of AIM. Instead, it has been suggested that this service charge should be waived or kept to a minimum to honour the spirit of *qard hassan*, such that this is offered to the hard-core poor only. The issue here is that in the public eye, offering a loan in the form of *qard-hasan* while charging a service fee (*ujrah*) resembles a conventional loan provided by any other commercial bank.

Additionally, other government agencies offering microfinance include Yayasan Usaha Maju, which primarily provides loans to the poor and hard-core poor in Sabah, and The Economic Fund for National Entrepreneurs Group (TEKUN), which was established under the Ministry of Agriculture and Agro-Based Malaysia to provide easy and quick loans to Bumiputra and Indian entrepreneurs.

Besides those, several private financial institutions (PFIs) offer microfinancing plans which enable fast, easy and convenient access to business financing of up to RM50,000 without collateral. These plans have been supporting the financing needs of micro-enterprises since 2006 under the National Sustainable Microfinance framework.

---

micro credit financing to support business activities which can raise revenue.

Micro-enterprises can access financing at a lower rate channelled through PFIs, from the Micro-Enterprise Fund established by the Central Bank of Malaysia.

Despite such a vibrant ecosystem of microfinancing opportunities, challenges remain in poverty alleviation efforts through the provision of microfinance. From the demand side, some poor households are still averse to borrowing from these plans. Factors for this include a lack of confidence, skills, knowledge and business acumen, the high credit risk, and the ability to balance running a business with the struggle to survive against issues exacerbated by the pandemic.

From the supply side, Satar and Kassim (2020) argue that there is a lack of motivation and commitment by the staff of Islamic microfinance institutions to improve their understanding of economic principles and enhance the management of the institutions. There is also a lack in coverage, frequency, and effectiveness of business and financial management courses provided to their borrowers. Another specific challenge to Amanah Ikhtiar Malaysia (AIM) is long-term dependency on government subsidies, which puts the fund's sustainability and continuity into question.

All in all, there is certainly room for improvement in terms of enhancing the effectiveness and efficacy of microfinancing schemes. It is also important to emphasize that increased access to microfinance seeks to propel social mobility through sustainable income generation from business activities. As such, there needs to be a graduation mechanism in place to prevent those who have broken out of the poverty cycle from continuously depending on these schemes. Otherwise, it will become a dependency handicap for the recipients while excluding those who are truly in need, in addition to becoming financially unsustainable for the institution in the long term.

Part II

Addressing Urban Poverty

Introduction

RECOGNIZING THE STATUS of urban poverty in Malaysia and analysing the gaps in the field is just the necessary starting point for proposing reforms that may help individuals move away from living in poverty. We will avoid as much as possible the use of expressions such as *eradication*, not because eradicating poverty is not a target worth attention, but because we want to avoid any utopistic approach to the issue.

Indeed, behind the word *eradication* we often find hidden different aid and subsidy programmes that focus on redistributing income and wealth; these represent policy makers' will – with its set of negative unintended consequences resulting from a poor trade-off analysis – rather than a sound and implementable vision. These programmes, which may provide temporary relief, do not address the fundamental nature of the problem; they provide help for a limited time, but they do not lift people out of poverty. Furthermore, they tend to nurture a dependence mentality, which is the greatest enemy in the fight against poverty.

With these policy recommendations we will shift the tone of the conversation from the idea of *poverty eradication* to one of *social mobility promotion*. **The key proposition will *not* be *to provide* urban poor with the resources**

they do not have, *but* **to promote reforms that can place them in the conditions** *to earn* **the resources they believe they need.**

Historical investigations suggests that for centuries poverty has been the normal condition for the majority of the population. Then in the 19th century something changed and *the Great Enrichment* began: from 1800 to the present the average person on the planet has been enriched in real terms by a factor of 10, or some 900 per cent (McCloskey, 2016).

The key element behind the great enrichment was *liberty*: a cultural and institutional framework promoting individual liberty that nurtured creative entrepreneurship and generated a true leap forward. In the sections below, we will see which initiatives can be taken from a policy perspective to promote *social mobility* by developing *entrepreneurship* through institutional and cultural changes.

At the same time, we wish to avoid the temptation of suggesting the creation of micro-enterprises; experience so far has shown that organizations created with entrepreneurial support schemes «are fragile enterprises, suggesting the priority may not simply be fostering higher levels of start-up activity among the poor, but interventions that enable them to become sustainable». Therefore, our goal is «the development of new insights on expanding opportunity horizons of these individuals, helping them escape the commodity trap, rethinking resourcing and microcredit, and assisting with adoption of the entrepreneurial mindset» (Morris, 2022).

II.1. The Framework:
Social Mobility through Entrepreneurship

II.1.1. Our Framework: Promoting Social Mobility through Entrepreneurship

How should we understand *entrepreneurship* in the present analysis?[1] Or, to put it better, what are the elements of entrepreneurial action that makes it so crucial and essential as a tool for promoting social mobility? Following Huerta de Soto (1992 and 2000), we would like to stress that the key element here is *creativity*; furthermore, creativity should be understood more broadly than simply as imagination applied to the creation of new products and their delivery to the market; indeed, a creative entrepreneurial action can also be linked with the discovery of new markets or raw materials, the introduction of new production processes, or the reorganization of an industry (Schumpeter, 1911); furthermore, creativity can also refer to the ability to connect markets and products by moving goods from where they abound to where they are scarce – being alert to unexploited profit opportunities (Kirzner, 1973). To summarize: entrepreneurship is innovative, and speculative creativity attempts to make good use of potential profit opportunities.

In a nutshell, entrepreneurial creativity can be defined as an attempt to develop a profitable organization by responding to market signals in a broader sense. In both arbitrage and innovative opportunities, entrepreneurs – in order to be successful – must fulfil a conscious or unconscious

---

1 While attempts have been made to theoretically define the concept of *entrepreneurship* (see, among others, Kirzner, 1973, Schumpeter, 1911 and Ferlito, 2020), here we will limit ourselves to a very broad approach to the category of entrepreneurial action in order to grasp the essential elements that can make entrepreneurship understood as a tool for social mobility.

need by providing a solution to the need that encounters market favour both in terms of its features and of its asking price.

It is quite curious that little space is devoted in economics textbooks to the category of entrepreneurship: markets are often described as engines, and their workings as that of a machine. Therefore, the feature of entrepreneurship is nowhere to be seen, and the entrepreneur disappeared along with it. This is a classic example of the huge dichotomy between the economy as it is understood by economists, the economy as it really is, and how it is perceived by laypeople. In fact, it is simply a matter of common sense to admit that the true protagonist in the marketplace is the entrepreneur, and that the market *process* is the emergent and evolving scenario set in motion by entrepreneurial decisions and their interactions with consumer choices.

Entrepreneurship is the main driver of the market process, and entrepreneurs are those who drive it forward. Entrepreneurial creativity belongs to human beings alone; this must be clear. There cannot be a category of entrepreneurship without entrepreneurs. We begin our discussion with this point, which is far from accepted by the dominant view, according to which markets are engines that can be regulated in order to achieve measurable-in-size policy targets. But here illusions must be broken: the market is not an engine. It is dominated by unpredictable individual actions and interactions – in turn driven by expectations – and there is no single omniscient mind able control and plan the kaleidic world of dispersed knowledge and constant change we live in. Government entrepreneurship can only be based on technical knowledge (knowing how to do things) that can be centralized and communicated – but that is static. In contrast, the relevant knowledge to make a plan successful in the market (knowing the conditions of time and place) is dispersed, non-transmissible and evolutionary. As such, this information dynamically arises only in the market, and it is communicated via the price system. Thus, entrepreneurship can be exercised only by individuals dynamically planning, acting and learning within the market process[2].

But why, for our current discussion, are entrepreneurial creativity and entrepreneurs so crucial? Are we not discussing the fight against poverty from the perspective of social mobility? Actually, the two topics are only apparently disconnected. Entrepreneurship is a crucial element in the fighting poverty for two reasons:

- Entrepreneurs are the only creators of true economic development and, therefore, of job opportunities.
- Under the proper educational and institutional framework, each of us exercises a certain degree of entrepreneurship that allows us to exploit our individual talents to move toward a situation in which we are better off.

Entrepreneurial creativity, which is purely a human feature, helps – we claim – in the fight against poverty. This is because it is the only force that can – and indeed does without rest – break the conditions of a stationary state, or of what it is called the 'evenly rotating economy' (or circular flow). On this point Schumpeter was very clear: an economic system develops only through the exercise of disruptive entrepreneurship. There is no economic development without entrepreneurial action, and without development the "pie" cannot grow, and therefore no opportunities are created.

---

2 The literature on the topic is extremely broad. Here we suggest referring to Hayek (1937, 1945), Mises (1920), Phaneuf (2020), Huerta de Soto (1992), Lavoie (1985a, 1985b).

Figure II.1 below, which refers to the United States, shows the negative correlation between entrepreneurship and the poverty rate: there is a negative and statistically significant relationship between poverty and entrepreneurship.

But how might one promote entrepreneurship? We believe that it cannot be taught at school, and a tax reform, although necessary (as discussed below), may be insufficient. A long-term strategy needs to be rooted in education and institutions.

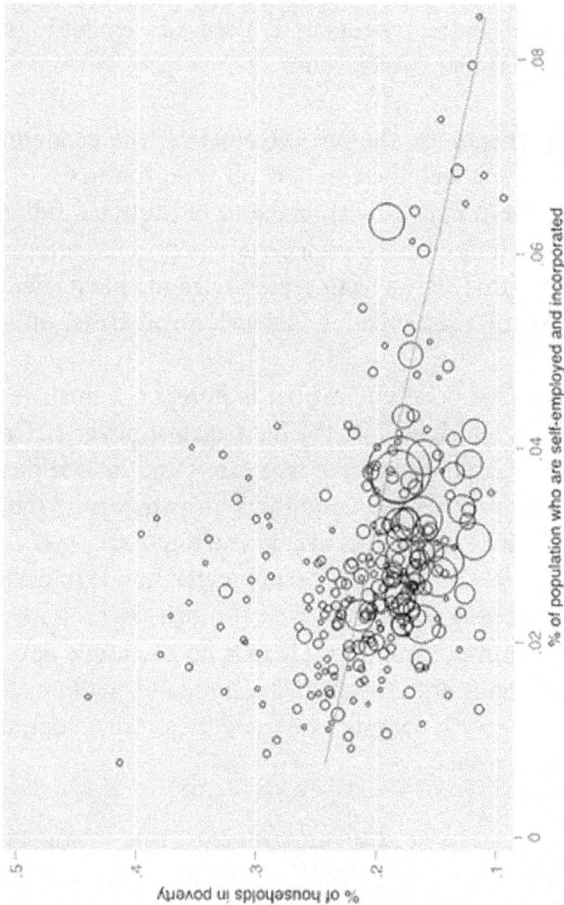

Figure II.1: Poverty vs. entrepreneurship in US metropolitan statistical areas, 2015.
Source: Lee and Rodríguez-Pose (2021, p. 39).

II.1.2. The Role of Institutions

What are institutions? The relevant literature distinguish-
es between «the "institutional environment" (society-wide
rules that often arise spontaneously) and "institutional
arrangements" (organizations that are usually the consequence of conscious design)» (Burns and Fuller, 2020, p.
577). Summarized succinctly, we may say that institutions
are «the formal and informal rules governing human behavior» (Boettke and Coyne, 2009, p. 139). Institutions,
then, constitute the rules of the game for human actions
and interactions; they contribute to generating economic
outcomes by providing incentives for different courses of
action.

The output that can potentially be produced by a certain
society at any point in time depends on «(1) the resources available, (2) existing technological knowledge, and, (3)
the existing institutional arrangement that either allows or
prevents the full and efficient use of the available resources.
Through the process of arbitrage, productive entrepreneurs
reallocate resources – physical resources as well as knowledge – to push the economy toward reaching the maximum
potential level of output [...]. Further, entrepreneurial innovation increases the amount of total output that an economy can potentially produce» (Boettke and Coyne, 2009,
pp. 156–157).

The proper institutional framework – Boettke and
Coyne (2009) contend – is the most important among the
three factors in order to generate a growth path emerging
from entrepreneurship. In this regard, there is broad agree-
ment that the institutions necessary for productive market
entrepreneurship are private property, low taxes, minimal
regulation, and constraints on government, although it is
not straightforward how those principles can be applied in

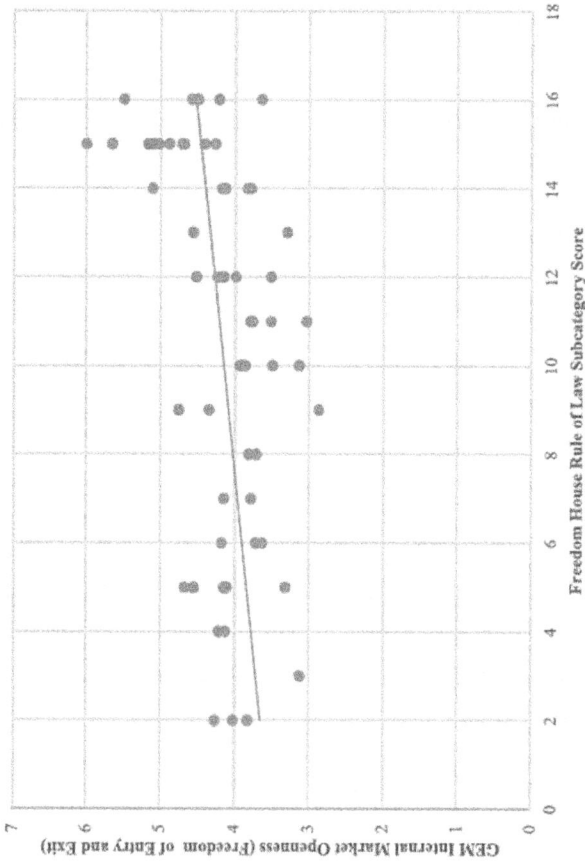

Figure II.3: Institutions and Productive Entrepreneurship. Source: Boettke and Candela (2017, p. 152).

a society in which they have not yet spontaneously emerged (Boettke and Coyne, 2009, p. 192).

Historically, it has been shown that

> human progress follows from the *generalized increasing returns* to commercial activity. These increasing returns follow from the gradual, cumulative process of *institutionalizing* the right to private property and freedom of contract under the rule of law. This path to liberty, and the generalized increasing returns that follow from it, generates a positive feedback loop. Through this feedback loop, additional norms emerge to reinforce the formal institutional framework of liberty. Once this cumulative process via generalized increasing returns reaches a critical tipping point, a "combustible combination" of Bourgeois commercial ideas, institutions, and commercial practices emerges. The emergence of this combustible combination in the early nineteenth century is what caused the explosive wealth creation and human flourishing that has taken place since then. The causal link between the path to liberty, as mentioned by Hayek above, and human progress that follows from it, is what Buchanan referred to as *generalized increasing returns* (Boettke and Candela, 2017, p. 138).

Furthermore, it has been demonstrated that a higher degree of rule of law and respect for property rights is conducive to more vibrant entrepreneurship activity.

So, if an environment of respect for well-defined property rights is a key factor in promoting entrepreneurship in the context of the competitive market process, and entrepreneurship promotion is a fundamental factor in the fight against poverty as we intend it, where does Malaysia stand in terms of institutional property rights support

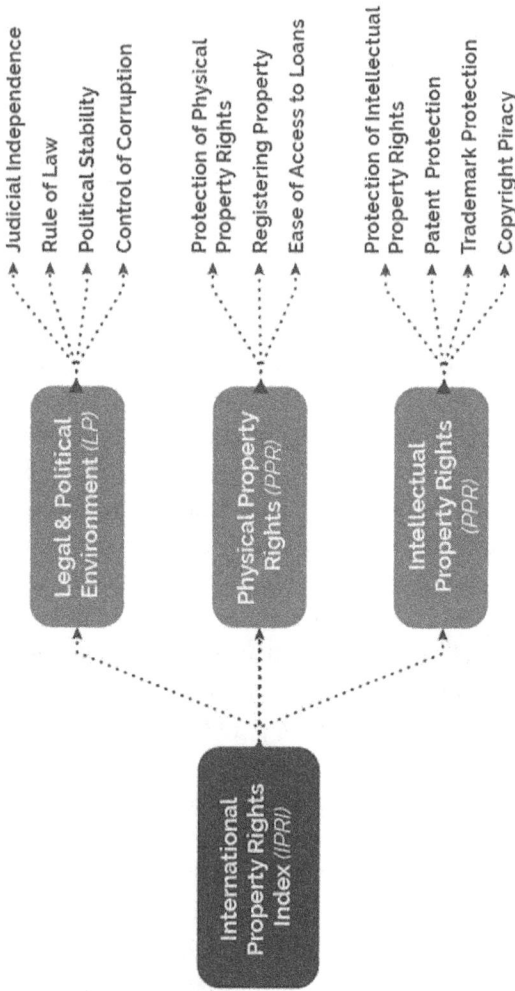

Figure II.4: International Property Rights Index Structure. Source: Levy-Carciente and Montanari (2021, p. 7).

ACCUMULATION OF LIBERTIES ->
INSTITUTIONALIZATION OF LIBERTY ->
GENERALIZED INCREASING RETURNS ->
HUMAN PROGRESS

Figure II.2: The path to human progress. Source: Boettke and Candela (2017, p. 138).

and a framework of liberty? For this we can refer to the work developed with the International Property Rights Index (IPRI) by the Property Rights Alliance in Washington, DC. (https://www.internationalpropertyrightsindex.org/).

The IPRI is made up of three levels and ten component. The report discusses the complete way of calculating each of the three components, and the IPRI is then calculated as (LP+PPR+IPR)/3.

In 2021, Malaysia's IPRI score decreased by -0.368 to 4.164, placing it 7th (out of 19 countries) in the Asia and Oceania region and 29th in the world (out of 129 countries). Malaysia's Legal and Political Subindex decreased by -0.16 to 2.831, with scores of 3.22 in Judicial Independence, 3.331 in Rule of Law, 1.166 in Political Stability, and 3.606 in Control of Corruption. Malaysia's Physical Property Rights Subindex decreased by -0.054 to 5.811, with scores of 4.313 in Perception of Property Rights Protection, 9.072 in Registering Property, and 3.886 in Ease of Access to Loans. Malaysia's Intellectual Property Rights Subindex decreased by -0.893 to 3.902, with scores of 4.057 in Perception of Intellectual Property Protection, 4.05 in Patent Protection, and 6.215 in Trademark Protection. Data wasn't available to measure Copyright Protection (https://www.internationalpropertyrightsindex.org/countries).

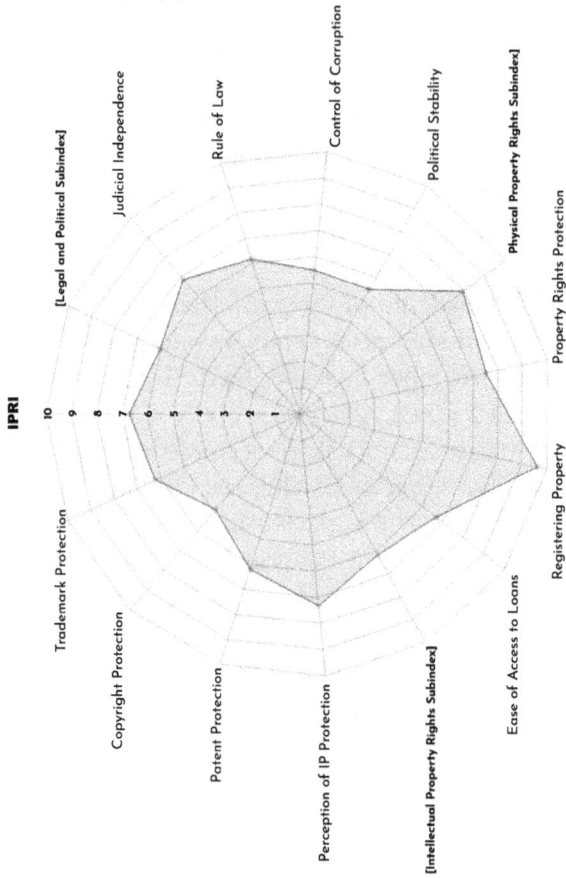

Figure II.5: Malaysia's IPRI 2021. Source: https://www.internationalpropertyrightsindex.org/country/malaysia.

While in 2021 the general IPRI score of Malaysia improved from 30th to 29th, it ranked only 42nd for Legal and Political Environment, 19th for Physical Property Rights and 32nd for Intellectual Property Rights. The details of the 2021 performances for the ten components can be observed in the figure below.

The evolution of the different three levels of the IPRI from 2007 to 2021 confirms that the weakest spot for Malaysia is the Legal and Political Environment.

It is rather interesting to observe that, in 2007 and 2008, Malaysia had quite a good score for the Legal and Political Environment, but the performance of that subset deteriorated quickly, and from 2009 onward it has remained the worst indicator for the country. Where does Malaysia presently stand regarding this problem?

As is shown in Figure II.7, while Malaysia has a problem in the general ranking for the Legal and Political Environment component of the IPRI, the most critical parts within the sub-component are political stability and control of corruption. Summarizing the other two sub-components, the strongest point for the PPR is registering properties, while the weakest is access to loans; for the IPR the strongest point is the perception of IP protection, and the weakest is actual copyright protection.

In conclusion, in order to develop an institutional environment with a higher degree of property rights definition and recognition, which would be an important driver for entrepreneurship and therefore for the fight against poverty, Malaysia needs to enact reforms in the following areas:

- Promoting political stability;
- Fighting corruption;
- Improving access to loans;
- Higher copyright protection.

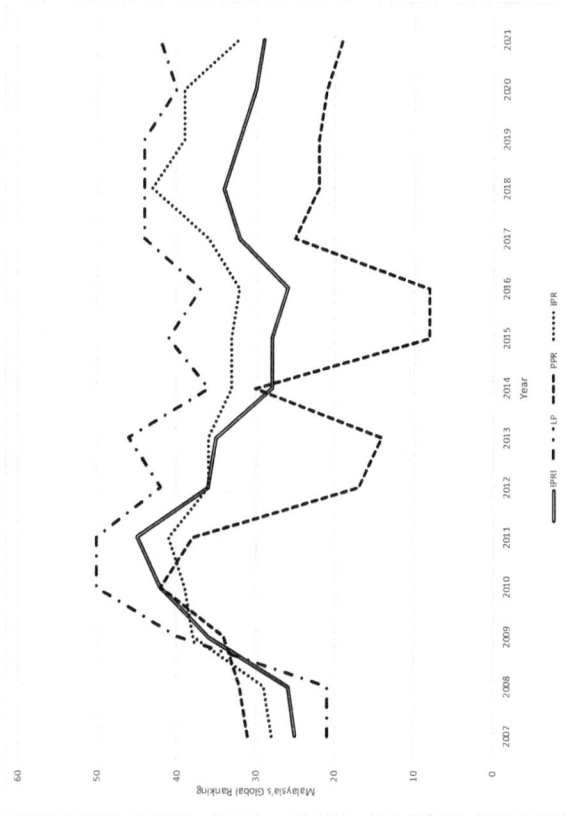

Figure II.6: Malaysia's IPRI components – 2007–2021. Source: Our re-elaborations on https://www.international-propertyrightsindex.org/country/malaysia.

II.1.3. Reforming Education

At the micro-level, the right institutions are the emergent product of a cultural system; therefore, education reform is one of the policy levels at which we can operate in order to achieve the targets described above (a higher degree of property rights support, conducive to entrepreneurship).

While the debate about Malaysia's education is often focused on which language should be used for which discipline, such a focus misses an important target we should take into account. In fact, we believe that the major flaw of the current education system is its strong imbalance between sciences and humanities; while an important emphasis is placed on mathematics and engineering, the humanities – such as literature, philosophy, history and geography – are taught in a way that is often unable to help students grasp the bigger picture about the world they live in.

While mathematics and engineering are important disciplines to provide students with technical skills, they are not enough to nurture the critical thinking that is so urgently needed to awaken a domestic and creative answer to the challenges posed by the present scenario (entrepreneurial spirits); the history of those disciplines shows precisely just how much history is important for the sciences too. How is it possible to grasp Malaysia's place in a globalized world if world history is not comprehensively taught? Understanding the present conditions of time and place requires knowledge of how those very conditions evolved. As an example, the presence of tin mines cannot be ignored to understand the role of the British in Malaysia, and knowing that history is crucial to understanding present day Malaysia. And how is possible to understand globalization without knowing the history and the geography of the spice trade routes and their political context?

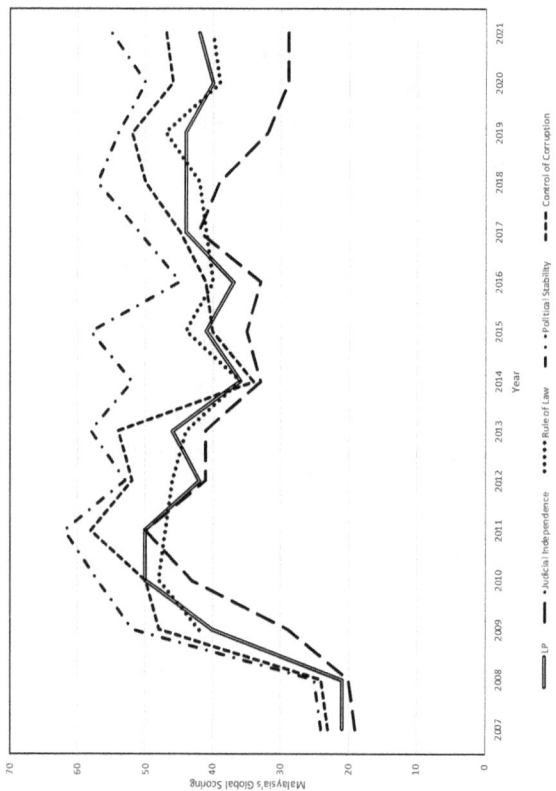

Figure II.7: Malaysia's Legal and Political Environment Component in the IPRI – 2007–2021. Source: Our re-elaborations on https://www.internationalpropertyrightsindex.org/country/malaysia.

History and geography expose students to the evolution of the conditions of time and place so they may grow in their understanding of where we are now. At the same time, the knowledge of literature and philosophy places students in close touch with those authors who, over centuries, built not only our culture but also our very system of thought: although unconsciously, we all use thought categories that were defined by Plato and Aristotle more than 2300 years ago. If you wish to challenge the common way of doing things, how can you ignore the works of those who did all this this before you?

These principles need to find immediate application in a reformed primary school, where today not enough emphasis is dedicated to acquiring a balanced and systematic knowledge of humanist subjects. During the last year of primary school, a special program should be provided to help students in choosing their future study path according to the courses offered by secondary schools. The program should aim to help students in finding their vocation, in close coordination with their families.

In order to nurture the process of self-discovery and to enrich each student's personal growth path, secondary education should no longer be understood as "generalist". We suggest introducing different educational paths, because colleges and universities should not be reduced to high-level secondary schools; this would allow them to truly flourish in pursuing their fundamental cultural mission, because the students they welcome will have already received the necessary education to access the academic world and treat it for what it is: a centre for developing high culture.

It is only natural that not all students will want to attend a tertiary education system designed to be deeply intellectual and academic. This is the reason why the secondary education paths we propose should train people for various

professions. An example may make things more under-
standable: accounting can be taught in secondary school,
and someone who desires to be an accountant could enter
the job market after secondary school without the need to
graduate from college; universities, instead, should not focus on the professions, but rather concentrate only on those
who wish to have access to jobs in which a higher level of
academic skills is required.

This reform will also help in lowering the level of
post-graduation frustration; in fact, as nowadays everybody has access to tertiary education (intended however
as a higher level of secondary education, but not seriously
academic), everybody expects to get a top job after graduation. This is unrealistic, as the job market will always remain shaped as a pyramid. The process of self-knowledge
implied in the education world we envisage would help students understand how they can fully develop themselves
with regard to their own traits and be of service to the common good.

The two main achievements of such an education reform in relation to social mobility would be:

• Faster access to the professional market for those individuals who do not intend to pursue tertiary education,
  and therefore faster access to financial resources and,
  potentially, more rapid career advancement;
• The enhancement of critical thinking, thanks to a higher
  degree of humanist knowledge: creativity, the essence of
  entrepreneurship, implies challenging the status quo.

II.1.4. Reshaping the Growth Model

The emergence of new entrepreneurial forces can be a
source of social mobility not only at the *micro* level, via

the creation of income resources for people, but also at the *macro* level, by changing the growth model, which today in Malaysia appears to be unbalanced and unsustainable.

In fact, while most analysts look at GDP as a whole, positive performance per se is not a sufficient reason to be optimistic. In fact, not all the GDP components "are born equal" and, *ceteris paribus*, some of them can generate unsustainable growth. Here it is worth recalling the half-century old warning by the German economist Ludwig M. Lachmann (1973, p. 36):

> Discussions on matters of economic growth have become a favourite pastime of our age. Among newspaper readers and television viewers all over the world, even among some economists, the notion that in this great age of ours it has become possible to sum up in one single figure the result of the economic activity of groups of individuals in countries, regions, or industries, appears to be accepted as a self-evident truth. Such figures are then used as a measure for comparisons over time and, with gusto, between countries. In many circles a low rate of growth of the gross national product has come to be regarded as a symptom of a social malaise.

To continue using Lachmann's jargon, GDP analyses and forecasts, to be useful, require hermeneutics, or interpretation. A simple example will make the point: if, *ceteris paribus*, the government devotes resources to unproductive expenditures and, furthermore, these outlays are financed by printing or borrowing money, then statistics will show an increase in GDP, but the consequences of how GDP was increased will most likely be inflation and unemployment. In a nutshell, the microfoundations behind macro-aggregates matter more than the aggregates themselves.

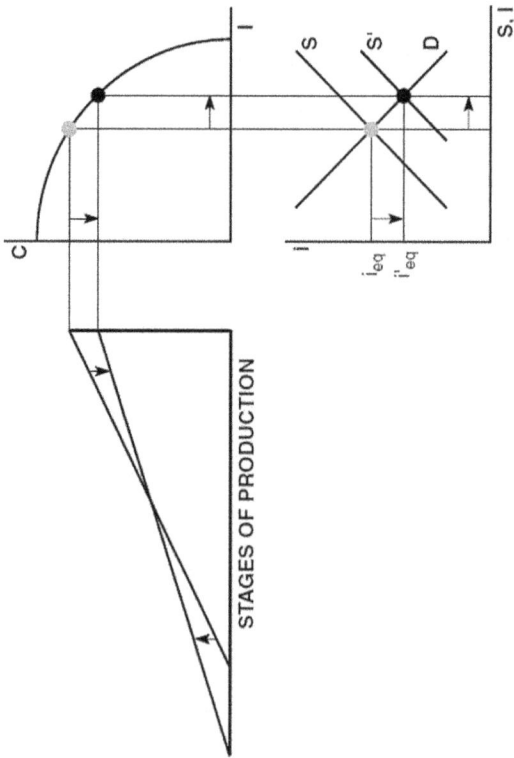

Figure II.8: A restructuring of capital induced by the increase in saving (change occurring in time preferences).
Source: Garrison (2001, p. 62).

The real economic challenge for Malaysia, therefore, is not the growth of GDP per se, but a shift in the growth model. For 2022, while still expecting strong private consumption (+9% in 2022), Bank Negara Malaysia foresees a stronger pace for investments than in the past, both private (+5.3%) and public (+9.6%). However, we may encounter a dichotomy here: long-term sustainable growth is based on investments financed by the existence of real savings, and savings are the counterpart of consumption. Therefore, the combination for long-term sustainable growth is made up of investments and savings, rather than investments and consumption. In other words, in order to generate sustainable growth, an increased demand for loanable funds to be destined to investments needs to be preceded by increased thriftiness among consumers (Garrison, 2001, p. 62).

In such a situation, when savings rise, the (equilibrium, or natural) interest rate tends to fall.

Figure II.8 describes the process of sustainable growth fed by a modification in time preferences. Consumers are more future-oriented, making more loanable capital available through the increase in savings. This is reflected in a movement of the savings supply to the right (from S to S', lower quadrant on the right). Naturally, in the capital market this is reflected by a fall in the interest rate (from i_{eq} to i'_{eq}), with a consequent increase in demand for investment funds (downward movement of the point of equilibrium on curve D). This change can be projected on the PPF graph (top quadrant on the right), where one can see how a decrease in consumption frees up resources for investment. The lowest level of consumption can in turn be projected onto Hayek's triangle[3] (top quadrant on the left): its height

---

3 Hayek's Triangle was introduced by Hayek (1931, p. 39). The base of the triangle is the production period. The height measures the value of the final consumption goods produced during the production process.

(consumption level) will be reduced, while the hypotenuse becomes flatter, thereby demonstrating the lengthening of the production period due to the increased level of investments in time-consuming projects (Ferlito, 2013, p. 84).

The policy agenda for putting Malaysia's recovery on solid ground needs to be based on the following pillars:

- Restoring saving capacity (tackling household debt);
- Relaunching private investments.

In conclusion, GDP growth is not significant if not based on the right pillars – investments and savings – which can drive the country toward sustainable growth, rather than growth per se. In fact, without proper attention to the microfoundations, a perilous path of unsustainable growth and a boom-and-bust cycle can be initiated.

Thus, enhancing entrepreneurship will not only help individuals, but – as a positive unintended consequence – will also shift the country's growth model toward a sustainable path (centred on a virtuous relationship of savings/investments) and away from the current unsustainable path (centred on a debt/consumption vicious cycle).

The various vertical distances between the hypotenuse and the axis of time are the values of the goods in production. A flatter hypotenuse signals a higher level of investments in long-term production processes (or more *roundabout* production methods, to use an expression coined by Boehm-Bawerk, 1884, Book I, Chapter 2).

II.2. Practical and Implementable Policy Recommendations

II.2.1. Housing Policy[4]

One of the fields where policy can play a more direct role in promoting social mobility is housing. So far, the Malaysian approach has been to provide homes to the poor at affordable rates; however, the outcome has been to promote the creation of low-quality housing areas that make the poor no less poor, just poor in a government-subsidised shelter. Again, our approach is instead to work so that the low-income segments of the population can move out of poverty (social mobility) and then decide if they want to buy or rent a housing unit according to their financial means. This implies also paying attention to location and connectivity as key factors in housing provision.

The issue, then, is not to promote home ownership (which would only further stress the already fragile financial situation of households), but to support social mobility: in this scenario, home ownership becomes an option, rather than a centrally planned policy target.

Here are some market-driven proposals to improve access to the housing market and, at the same time, promote social mobility.

II.2.1.1. Remove distortions from the supply side

One of the most fruitful efforts would be to focus on the removal of supply-side bottlenecks, in order to allow the supply to more easily adjust to the signals coming from the demand. As demonstrated by Hannah et al. (1989) with reference to the Malaysian case in the 1980s, the set

---

4 See Ferlito (2018, 2019).

of regulations involving the local property market is impeding the private sector from acting effectively in support of demand; this lack of action from the supply side is not only failing to provide shelter for low-income people, but it is also keeping prices on the high side because of demand pressure. Revision of the institutional framework «designed to increase the supply of low-cost units» should be designed in such a way as to increase the possibility for the supply to meet market preferences «by removing the cost distortions created by some of the legal minimum standards. The removal of those distortions stimulates developers to produce more low-income plots where the demand is the greatest, and not necessarily where land is the cheapest» (Bertaud and Malpezzi, 2001, p. 410). The last sentence emphasizes the very crucial fact that affordability is not only a matter of price, but also of location and size.

The issue of making the supply curve less inelastic is more critical than what is commonly understood. As argued by Malpezzi and Wachter (2005), «inelastic supply curves can give rise to "boom and bust" markets, and are the real cause of market instability, rather than "speculators"» (Malpezzi, 2014, p. 5). Malpezzi (2014, p. 5) also argues that such cycles are exacerbated «by badly designed government responses to rising housing prices by one-time programs to get the market moving, as in a "Million Houses Program;" [...] The analysis suggests it would be more effective to tackle rising prices by improving the efficiency of the supply of developable land, and real estate generally, including the development of an appropriate regulatory framework for real estate. Reform measures that tackle the root causes of inelastic supply have the effect of flattening the supply curve and moderating the boom and bust cycle, reducing risk for investors».

What are the factors in Malaysia that are presently

contributing to the inelasticity of the supply curve for affordable housing? First of all are the government agencies involved in the provision of affordable housing (see Ferlito 2018, pp. 26–27). Here the problem is not to reduce them from twenty to six, as proposed by the government, but rather that direct government action in the field will necessarily create obstacles to private attempts to enter that market segment. Moreover, such direct intervention usually does not take into account the affordability trade-off of the three basic elements (price, size, location).

In a less evident but equally distortionary way, other regulations are impeding the mode and speed of an adequate private supply of affordable housing by private developers; I should mention here the bumiputra quotas in low-cost housing projects and the compulsory affordable housing quotas for private developers. Both these measures impede supply moving in the direction signalled, via the price mechanism, by demand. Similarly, and as previously discussed, all the excessively strict requirements that surround building affordable homes, such as minimum size, impede sound coordination between supply and demand; furthermore, they have regressive effects, and in the medium run they can limit general economic growth.

The same considerations apply to the extra regulatory costs created by different forms of subsidies (Hannah et al., 1989, pp. 59–60). Our suggestion here is that government agencies involved in the provision of homes should be frozen in their power to act. Similarly, all the other elements limiting the elasticity of the housing supply and the involvement of private developers in the low-end segment, such as the bumiputra quotas and the time-consuming and contradictory regulations or minimum size requirements, should be quickly removed to allow supply and demand to react faster to signals coming from the price system, as well as to allow people to freely make better choices for themselves when facing tradeoffs between price, floor space, and location.

We wish to be clear on this point: the low-end market segment is not disregarded by private developers because it is *naturally* unprofitable, but because it is *artificially* made unprofitable by the regulatory obstacles mentioned above.

II.2.1.2. The importance of creative destruction

The current national housing policy suggests that the government is aware of the positive effect that technological development can exercise to lower prices. However, the process of technological development, which, following Schumpeter (2011), becomes innovation when applied to the production process, is not something that can be developed *ex-cathedra* via central planning.

The phenomenon of creative destruction, the competition between the emergence of something new in the economic system and the struggle for survival by what is old, is the essential fact of capitalist development. The battle for new elements (new products, new markets, new methods of productions, etc.) to emerge happens in the market and, in the market, it is accompanied by a downward movement of prices. In order to be carried out, innovations need special types of people – entrepreneurs – that are, first and foremost, alert to unexploited profit opportunities (Kirzner, 1973).

However, such alertness can only be exercised in the market due to the signalling role played by the price mechanism; for this very reason, entrepreneurship – the response to stimuli arising in the market – cannot be planned by any single player outside it.

If technological development applied to affordable

housing is welcomed, in order to emerge it requires a high degree of entrepreneurial freedom to maneuver so that market signals can be captured by alert entrepreneurs. Thus, from a policy perspective the role of government should not be that of an entrepreneur – this would be ontologically impossible, because governments operate outside the market – but to remove obstacles, such as transaction-cost barriers and direct business involvement, which might disincentivize the formation of new businesses (Gjerstad and Smith 2014, p. 245). This would help the economic system seek its path toward a capital reorganization consistent with such new possibilities and avoid blocking resources in industries which do not offer profit opportunities.

II.2.1.3. A new role for the rental market

We believe that the rental market will play a growing role in the Malaysian market in the future, and not for merely economic considerations; we also base our analysis on cultural factors that are often disregarded in policy discussions, but that can be decisive in understanding the complexity under examination. From a purely economic perspective, it is easy to understand that, since Malaysia is on a fast track to become a developed country, it is not realistic to expect that housing prices will be where they were before the development process. We should not forget that between 1976 and 1982 housing prices rose by an average of 18.6 per cent per annum, and in the same period household income rose by only 10.8 per cent per annum (Hannah et al., 1989, p. 6); the current dynamics seem less discouraging, with salaries growing faster than housing prices. In the present evolutionary scenario, the housing market should be analyzed by considering it as a whole, including an increasing role for the rental market.

As demonstrated by preliminary studies on the evolution of spending habits, the generations currently entering the housing market from the demand side are living between the cultural pressure from previous generations about the importance of saving for and buying a property as soon as possible and the new, more present-oriented and dynamically evolving mentality that emphasizes the role of entertainment expenditures, such as those devoted to travelling or new communication devices.

In such an evolutionary scenario, while rent-to-own schemes are welcome and deserve to be incentivized, a different role might be conceived for the government in facing the shelter issue. A solution that overcomes the problems created by subsidies, vouchers and direct government housing investments is the so-called guaranteed-rent method, suggested by Jacobs (1961, pp. 326–331). This is a way to introduce «new construction gradually instead of cataclysmically, of introducing new construction as an ingredient of neighborhood diversity instead of as a form of standardization, of getting new private construction into blacklisted districts and of helping to unslum slums more rapidly» (Jacobs, 1961, p. 326). With the implementation of this method, the «physical units involved would be buildings, not projects – buildings to go among other buildings, old and new, on city streets. These guaranteed-rent buildings would be of different kinds and sizes, depending on their kind of neighborhood, the size of the plot, and all such considerations as normally influence the size and type of more or less average dwellings» (Jacobs, 1961, p. 326).

The system of guarantees suggested by Jane Jacobs would move in two directions. In case the developer is able to get a loan through the traditional financial market, the government (or one of its agencies) would guarantee the mortgage; in case the developer fails to do so, the public authority would become the money lender. The second action from the government side is to «guarantee to these builders (or to the owners to whom the buildings might subsequently be sold) a rent for the dwellings in the building sufficient to carry them economically» (Jacobs, 1961, pp. 326–327). In exchange, the builder would be required to select tenants from the group of people designated by the government agency in charge. By examining the applicant's income, the agency would decide how much of the economic rent could actually be paid and make up the difference; if «a household's income improved, its proportion of the rent would go up, and the proportion provided by the subsidy would go down. If and when a household reached the point of paying a full economic rent, it would thereafter – for as long as this was true» be no concern for the public authority (Jacobs, 1961, pp. 327–328).

The most important difference with a traditional program of public housing is that with the guaranteed-rent method the capital costs are not directly borne by government; with this system, they would be kept in the rent equation when defining the total economic rent to be received by the builder. Real estate taxes could also be incorporated in the rent determination (Jacobs, 1961, p. 329). Moreover, the agency in charge should not be involved in the details regarding construction standards; such a choice would be left to developers and determined by market conditions.

Such a solution implies a lower financial burden for the government, a burden that would decrease if the households renting these units improve their economic conditions. This would be all the more true and likely to happen if no restrictive barriers were imposed on location. This would create the possibility for the poor to choose dwellings closer to the economic heartbeat of a city, increasing their chances for social mobility. At the same time, the risk of the emergence of slums devoted to poor people, in locations that would ultimately keep them poor, would be avoided, or at least drastically diminished.

II.2.2. Tax Reform: Less income tax, more consumption tax, decentralization

We will not discuss here a general proposal for reforming the Malaysian tax system[5]; we will only focus on those reforms that may be useful for more directly addressing poverty and promoting social mobility.

Earlier in this section, we discussed the importance of shifting the growth model, now unbalanced in favour of consumption, toward a more saving/investment oriented path. The fiscal proposals presented here are an attempt to nudge in the same direction.

II.2.2.1. A lower income tax

Due to the new taxes proposed below, it will be necessary to adjust the burden of direct income taxation, as merely adding fiscal burdens will disincentivize economic activity and thus have a depressing effect. In fact, the need for the government to improve its revenues would be frustrated if such an attempt were perceived as a limitation to economic activity.

In fact, as stated by Schumpeter (1918), we must refrain from developing a tax state in which the fiscal burden grows to sustain the very system that supports the tax mechanism. «A bigger and bigger army of bureaucrats is needed to enforce the tax laws, tax inquisition becomes more and more intrusive, tax chicanery more and more unbearable. The

---

5 The Center for Market Education presented a comprehensive tax reform in Singh (2021).

absurd waste of energy that this picture entails shows that the meaning of the organization of the tax state lies in the autonomy of the private economy, and that this meaning is lost when the state can no longer respect this autonomy».

We propose here to lower the income tax, both on individuals – for whom it should become even flatter – and on corporations. The reform should be a combination of modified rates and higher exemption thresholds for the lower income groups. We suggest that for the actual details the government should engage with the relevant stakeholders. The aim of the proposal is to help all income earners, in particular those from the lower groups, to cope with the new GST proposed below.

At the same time, we must avoid developing a large system, because it would be a source of inefficiencies and complexities. As mentioned, a lower income tax should be also a flatter income tax (if not a totally flat one). Often, taxation is complex and inefficient because it is large. According to Garrison (1996, p. 674), «the smaller the tax, the greater the prospects for simplicity and efficiency. And a flat rate may be the best means of keeping a small tax from becoming a big one».

A shift toward indirect taxation can help improve collection, but it must be accompanied by higher standards of enforcement for both direct and indirect taxes and by the reduction of unnecessary government expenditures.

II.2.2.2. Introducing the Targeted-GST

The reduction of the income tax should be partially replaced by a consumption tax. With the Pakatan Harapan victory, the previous GST was abolished and replaced by the SST. However, we believe that the way in which the GST was designed was more effective both in terms of implementation from the business side and of collection by the government. Moreover, being a fiscal credit for purchasers at each stage except the last one, it presented a lighter effect on final prices. Our proposal, therefore, goes in the direction of re-introducing the GST but with some differences. At the same time, the SST should be abolished.

From our perspective, the case for a consumption tax mainly lies in the possibility of stimulating household saving in a country – Malaysia – burdened by a very high household debt.

Against this proposal one may argue that taxing consumption could have a regressive effect, which means that the relative burden would be higher on the lower income citizens. This would be all the more true with regard to those basic goods which constitute the purchasing basket of the low-income population. This is why we suggest a progressive consumption tax; however, such progressivity should not be designed in such a way as to frustrate productive initiatives and luxury consumption, which are key elements for economic growth. The unintended consequence of an overly progressive approach would be to discourage consumption behaviours that benefit the entire economic system; it should not be forgotten that to 'punish' certain types of consumption would affect the production of the goods involved, bringing harm to the relative value chain and its workers. Our proposal is as follows:

- exempted goods: items related to the basic consumption habits of the lower-income population, such as rice;
- low-rate GST (3%): key development items, such as culture and education-related goods;
- middle-rate GST (6%): all goods not identifiable within the other three categories;
- high-rate GST (10%): luxury goods.

The rates indicated above should be intended as a suggestion, indicating the direction we believe to be beneficial;
such a suggestion remains open for discussion.

What are the advantages of a consumption-centered
tax reform that reduces income tax and introduces instead
a consumption tax? As mentioned, our proposal moves in
the direction of promoting an investment-led growth model, and a necessary condition for an investment-led growth
is the existence of savings.

Thus from our perspective, the case for a consumption
tax lies mainly in the possibility of stimulating saving. The
presence of a higher amount of savings can support the
demand for loanable funds coming from future-oriented
investors.

The effect of such a reform would be represented first
and foremost by a variation of PPF in the private sector (see
Figure II.9). In fact, a tax on consumption obviously leads
to a modification of the structure of intertemporal preferences, thereby facilitating the creation of savings. The structure of preferences becomes more oriented towards the future, thereby generating resources for private investment,
thanks to increased savings.

> The consumption intercept will move toward the origin,
> reflecting reduced after-tax consumption possibilities; the
> investment intercept will move away from the origin, re-
> flecting tax-free investment possibilities. Equivalently, the
> generally decreased slope of the PPF reflects the fact that
> tax reform of this sort changes the intertemporal trade-off
> in favour of investment (Garrison, 2001, pp. 102–103).

So, what may be seen is an increase in both savings (the
supply of loanable funds) and investments (the demand for
loanable funds): there is an acceleration of the economic

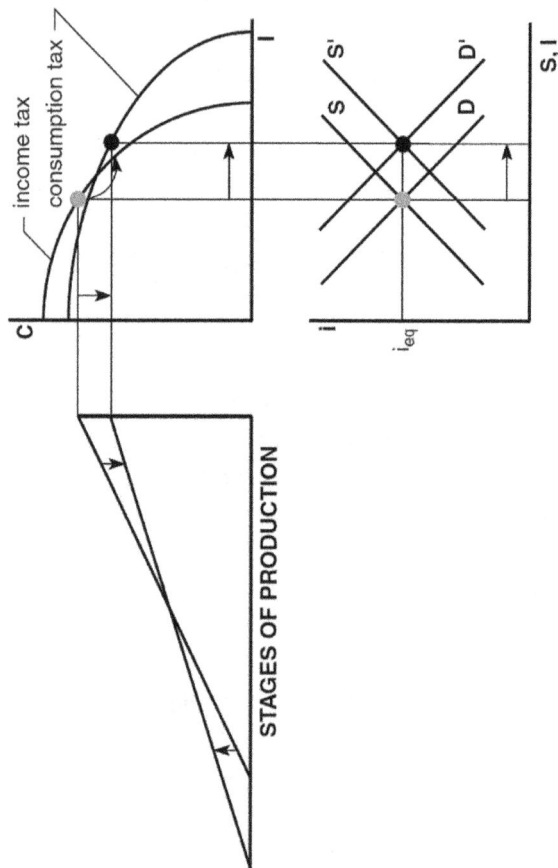

Figure II.9: The effects of a tax reform shifting from income to consumption tax. Source: Garrison (2001, p. 103).

system's growth rate; «the increased growth due to tax re-form is sustainable growth» (Garrison, 2001, p. 104).

The key item, therefore, is not tax reform *per se* but the possibility of reducing consumption without changing the interest rate, while allowing a natural change in the structure of time preferences. Garrison (2001, p. 104) emphasizes that «it is precisely the reduction of consumption that makes a higher growth rate possible». Following this perspective, it consequently becomes undeniable that the common idea whereby growth is generated by stimulating consumption is completely false, because stimulating consumption during the transition by means of, say, a transfer expansion may be counter-productive. Again, if the net effect of the transitional dipping down and of the transfer expansion is actually to leave consumption spending unchanged, then the supposed beneficial effects of more rapid growth would be negated (Garrison, 2001, p. 105).

Reintroducing the GST can also become an occasion to test the possibility of a higher degree of tax devolution, with the local states more involved in tax collection so that they may have more directly access to funds that can be used to support the territory. We propose the T-GST be collected by the state; while 20% of it would be retained by the state, 80% would be transferred to the federal government. A higher amount of funds available at the local level would allow designing better-informed anti-poverty schemes centered on actual territorial conditions, which are more likely to be known by government levels closer to citizens.

II.2.2.3. A progressive capital gain tax

Another way to support the low-income segments of the population is to mitigate cyclical fluctuations. The proposal

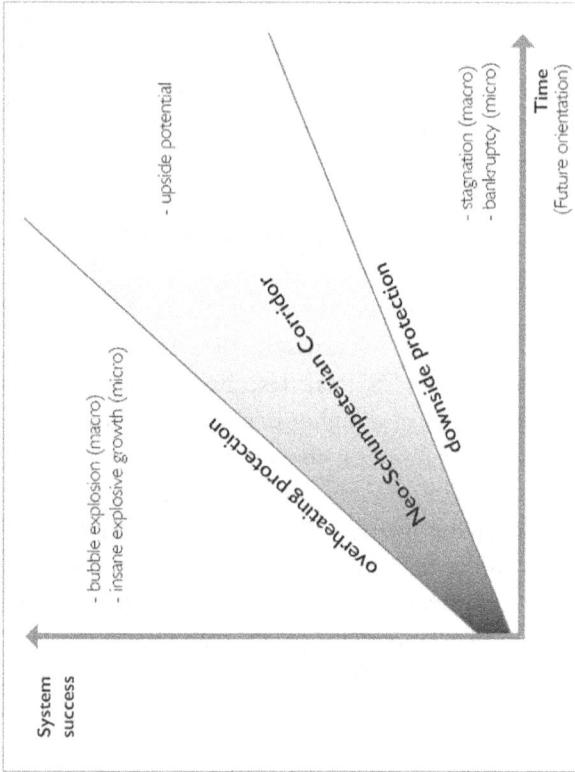

Figure II.10: Neo-Schumpeterian Corridor. Source: Hanusch and Wackermann (2011, p. 64).

for a progressive capital gain tax is part of the public sector role in supporting the healthy growth of the economy.

We would like to label this proposal as the 'Hanusch-Wackermann tax' (from now on HWT), because, as far as we are aware, it was proposed for the first time with anti-cyclical purposes in Hanusch and Wackermann (2011).

Hanusch and Wackermann (2011, pp. 61–62) described the economic system as an organic body in which development is brought in by the interaction of the three pillars that constitute this body: industry, finance and the public sector. Their proposal for a progressive capital gain tax is considered as part of the public sector role in supporting healthy growth of the economy, a role that «should be guided by a two-sided counter-cyclical strategy: on the one hand the concern to avoid trends of exaggerating or overheating in time and on the other hand the responsibility and effectiveness to overcome a possible period of stagnation as quickly as possible» (Hanucsh and Wackermann, 2011, p. 63). The HWT, as we shall soon see, would help the economic system in growing within the boundaries of what the authors call the *Neo-Schumpeterian Corridor*.

As explained in Hanusch and Wackermann (2011, p. 65), the idea «of such a corridor presupposes that the political sphere can [...] take the appropriate measures that can effectively and opportunely tame and dominate those forces in a capitalistic system which continuously try to go through the roof and risk exiting the corridor towards an excessive growth path». At the same time, policy makers «have to make sure that an economy will not fall out of the corridor, and that it will not have to cope with economic stagnation».

Probably nobody has better described than Schumpeter the conflict that can happen between innovative and strongly growing industries and slowly developing sectors in a dynamically growing market economy; he summarized that conflict with the famous expression "creative destruction". In such a scenario, the more dynamic industries attract «the attention and interest of all those economic actors who desire to participate in the boom in fast-growing domains as financial investors, and who will also want to enjoy the high returns achievable» (Hanusch and Wackermann, 2011, p. 66). The role of expectations and of the financial markets – described in the first paragraph – return here as generators of a «finance-based overheating that can topple the whole economy into a severe crisis» (Hanusch and Wackermann, 2011, p. 66). As explained by Minsky's financial instability hypothesis (Minsky, 1982 and 2008), during a boom following a period of tranquillity «innovative debt practices and speculative excesses» are encouraged and an «unrecognized system fragility evolved» (Prychitko, 2010, p. 206).

How can a progressive capital gain tax help keep the system moving within the corridor without limiting the positive effects produced by profit-seeking behaviours? According to Hanusch and Wackermann (2011, pp. 68–69), this tax could be an automatic stabilizer to investment behaviour. As it is easy to implement, the proposed scheme would create a situation in which the lower the return, the lower the tax rate. It is well known that, in general, low return investments also have low risk, and consequently such a tax would favour conservative behaviour.

"Overall, we would see a shift in the behavior away from highly speculative investments promising a high rate of return, because some investors will lose interest because of the increased tax burden. In a situation where the economy finds itself above the corridor, fewer people will join the bandwagon, and the dangerous bubble formation might evolve at a slower speed. This would give the system the chance to slow down on its own or integrate the highly dynamic sectors in such a way as to widen bottlenecks before a looming breakdown.

"In times when the economy is stagnating and below the neo-Schumpeterian corridor, the low tax rates incite investors to leave their money in the capital market and support a sustainable development. [...]

"Furthermore, the government would increase its tax receipts above average in boom times due to the rising tax rates and could, theoretically, use the money to support the economy in times when it nevertheless falls through the corridor" (Hanusch and Wackermann, 2011, pp. 69–70).

With this scheme, innovative industries may still attract investors at the beginning of their expansion, when expected returns are low and financial resources are more needed, while the influx of second-comer speculators may be contained precisely because they tend to enter the game when returns are rising and therefore they could be discouraged, at least to a certain extent, by increasing taxation. Thus, less money is invested when returns are on the rise and speculation-induced overheating could be prevented. Anti-cyclicality is then built into the scheme (Hanusch and Wackermann, 2011, p. 71).

II.2.2.4. Introducing Percentage Tax Designation Institutions

What happens when we, as taxpayers, have the freedom to choose how to spend a share of our tax money, that is, where to allocate it or whom to give it to? *Percentage Tax Designation Institutions* (PTDIs), also known as 'Percentage

Philanthropy Laws', are fiscal institutions through which taxpayers can freely designate a certain percentage of their income tax to entities whose main activity is of public interest: religious organizations, worship places, third-sector organizations, political parties, etc. PTDIs came into force in some Southern and Central-Eastern European countries – Italy, Spain, Portugal, Hungary, Romania, Poland, Slovakia and others – many years ago.

As explained by Paolo Silvestri (2019), this particular tax institution is one of the forms of regulation that would be justified as a way of expanding opportunities for mutually beneficial transactions and, more particularly, as a liberal and contractarian approach to the provision of public goods.

Taking Italy as our reference example, we note that there are three different institutions through which taxpayers can allocate their taxes to public utility purposes: 1) 8x1000 (said as "8 per thousand"): designation to the state or a religious confession; 2) 5x1000: designation to the third sector and many other entities pursuing public utility purposes; 3) 2x1000: designation to political parties. Taxpayers can express their choice by signing a specific section of the tax return where they can also indicate the specific beneficiary of their tax money.

The way the choice can be made is regulated by a few basic rules that form what could be called the 'taxpayer's opportunity set'. This in turn can be understood as a decision-making process divided into several levels and sub-levels.

As explained by Paolo Silvestri, the implementation of such a fiscal mechanism empowers taxpayers, in the sense of allowing some discretion on the way in which public funds are spent. In fact, PTDIs could usefully be adapted to many cases in which there is divergence in people's beliefs about which kinds of public goods are valuable and which are not, in that each taxpayer can choose which fund on the list will receive his/her 0.8 per cent. At the same time, the system provides a rough and ready response to the free-rider problem, and it is also a way of ensuring that people contribute to the costs of only those public goods they actually value.

As example, it is clear that the system would be of valuable importance if we consider goods and services provided by religious confessions as public goods, and the disagreements among citizens(-taxpayers) over which religious confessions should be financed are not likely to be settled.

Furthermore, with this mechanism, the government is not subsidizing religious or other organizations according to its judgements about their relative merits; it is simply intermediating [mutually advantageous and agreeable] transactions in which individuals pay for activities they value.

The implementation of PTDIs could become the first step toward developing a new *Welfare Society* in which taxpayers are more an active than a passive party in the choice of how fiscal resources are spent to better society and provide public goods. The constant growth of 5x1000 funds in Italy testifies to how such a measure has encountered people's favour: in fact, people seem happy to decide how their taxes are spent, as they generally do not trust the traditional government-led allocative strategy.

It would be good to avoid a redistribution limit – which is present in the case of Italy – and to extend the freedom of choice not only to individual but to corporate taxpayers as well.

II.2.3. Liberalizing the labour market: ASEAN

One of the best ways to promote an entrepreneurial spirit

is *competition*. As one may easily understand, competition does not happen only between firms, but also among individuals, either within the same firm or at the general level of the economic system.

In Malaysia there has been a great deal of debate about foreign workers, who are cyclically accused of stealing jobs from the locals, thanks to foreigners' lower wage expectations. The reality during the Great Lockdown, however, has shown that unemployment and higher wages are not enough to attract Malaysian workers toward unskilled jobs; in fact many industries in the country cannot survive without recourse to foreign manpower.

The possibility of employers exploiting foreign workers has also been a topic of discussion. While better regulations on the conditions of unskilled workers are necessary, the current debate fails to appreciate that there is a shortcut which would help to both free foreign workers from the risk of exploitation and stimulate local workers' entrepreneurial skills: a total liberalization of individuals' movements within ASEAN, based on the example of what happens within the European Union.

Currently, ASEAN facilitates ASEAN tourists moving around the region for tourism or for short-term stays in general, while no discussion is open on the creation of an ASEAN job market. We propose allowing totally free movement of individuals within the region, so that job-seekers from an ASEAN country would be considered as local workers – without the need for special permissions – in all the other ASEAN countries.

This measure will surely support the conditions of migrant workers, as they could more easily change jobs, and therefore employers would need to compete – including with better wages – in order to keep the best workers with them.

However, for the scope of the present analysis, there are two ways in which such a reform would be supportive in the fight against poverty:

- With a higher degree of labour competition, Malaysian workers would receive a "natural" stimulus to improving their set of knowledge and skills; competition would nudge in favour of entrepreneurship;
- Malaysian workers would be exposed to the regional job market, and therefore they would have easier access to foreign countries in which their skills would be in demand and they could be judged as good fits.

Competition and a wider job market would then offer additional possibilities to the poor in order to improve their conditions according to the spirit of the present paper: not by giving them what they need, but by giving them more opportunities to earn what they believe to be appropriate.

II.2.4. Access to Credit

In the most recent years, Malaysia's score on the Access to Loans component of the International Property Right Index has improved.

However, the recent improvement is only a small step after a considerable deterioration in comparative terms from 2016 onwards. In fact, while Malaysia occupied the very first position in the ranking at the beginning of the 2010s, the relative scoring worsened in the second part of the decade.

Therefore, while improving in both absolute and relative terms, Malaysia needs to further push to return to a better ranking on the possibility for individuals and firms to have access to local financial services. This would also be important to spur entrepreneurship among the urban poor.

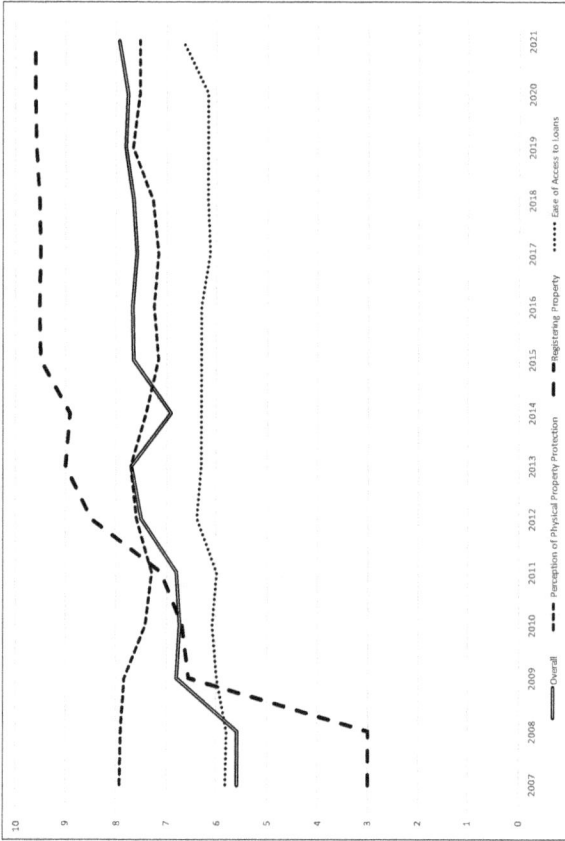

Figure II.11: Malaysia's Physical Property Rights scoring within the International Property Rights Index, 2007–2021.
Source: https://www.internationalpropertyrightsindex.org/country/malaysia.

However, when discussing microcredit and access to finance for the poor, in particular in urban contexts, most of the emphasis is placed on the possibility for people to support their daily expenditures or to purchase a car or a house, that is, on consumer credit: this is a limited approach to credit, as improving consumer credit per se can lead to situations of high household debt and high financial instability. That is precisely the case in Malaysia: household debt is consistently around 90% of GDP.

Instead, research has shown that a proper system of urban microfinance has considerable impact on poverty reduction, the standard of living, social well-being, empowerment, and entrepreneurship in the urban poor (Hasan et al. 2022).

In fact, the role of credit in the realm of entrepreneurship cannot be underestimated. The two aspects – entrepreneurial creativity and availability of financial means – cannot be separated. If the potential entrepreneur does not possess adequate financial capital, which is mostly the case if we consider the emergence of entrepreneurial spirits among the poor, those means need to be provided by a third party. According to Schumpeter (1911), financial institutions make entrepreneurial endeavors possible by the «creation of purchasing power».

However, in this regard it is important to move the discussion of credit in the realm of the fight against poverty away from the limiting scope of microfinancing:

Microfinance has meaningful, potentially transformative impacts for some entrepreneurs – especially those who, without microfinance, were stuck in a poverty trap. For other households, the effect is very small. In addition, microcredit induces some less-productive businesses to enter. This suggests that microlenders should consider more

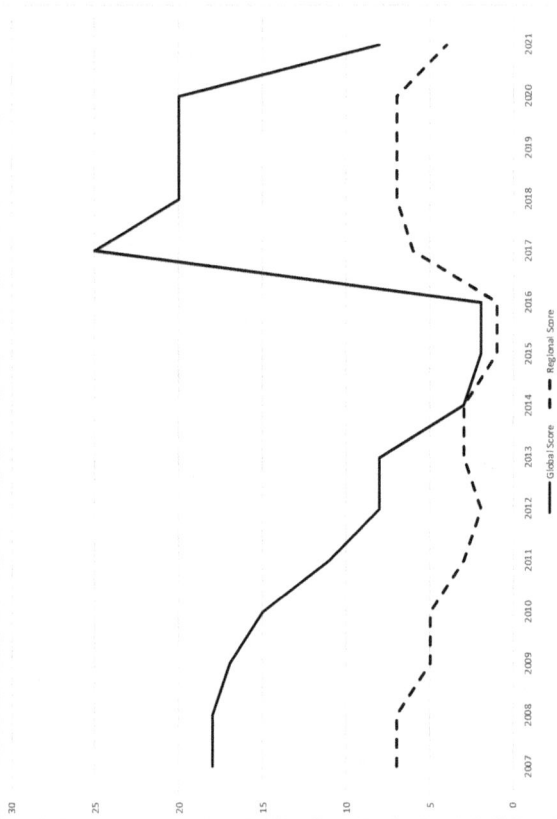

Figure II.12: Malaysia's Ease Access to Loans ranking, regional and global score, 2007–2021. Source: https://www.internationalpropertyrightsindex.org/country/malaysia.

screening of households in order to provide some larger loans. While limiting screening helps microlenders to reduce costs, it has a major downside: not channeling credit to where the effects would be largest. Given that new sources of data are now becoming available for lenders – for example, data from digital transactions, peers, and remote sensing – the ability to engage in more screening is increasing. Our results suggest it may be valuable to find ways to channel the right amounts of credit to those, like our 'gung-ho' entrepreneurs, who can make the best use of it (Banerjee et al., 2020).

While microcredit can be a necessary starting point and needs to be enhanced with new initiatives, we believe that a more holistic approach should be taken, beginning from the ground up. An often disregarded aspect in the discussion is that, in order for new potential entrepreneurs to have access to credit, *they must first exist*; while that statement may seem obvious, its purpose is to focus awareness on the fact that often microbusinesses emerging from the urban poor operate in the realm of the shadow economy and thus are not included in the available data. Their informal existence is an obstacle to accessing both social security measures and financing opportunities. Thus, the first measure that should be taken in this regard is to establish a special scheme for these entrepreneurial initiatives to emerge from the shadow economy. One system to do so is to induce these small firms to become registered in the formal economy system by introducing a forfeit tax system, whereby a small percentage would be paid on self-declared revenues; in exchange, the government should remove all other formal accounting fulfilments.

Bringing small firms into the light would be the first and necessary step to improving their access to credit markets.

The second recommended step would be to expand the credit market, allowing new, motivated competitors to enter the game and fight for market share by proposing new products. In this regard, awarding five digital banking licences in the first quarter of 2022 is set to provide a major boost to small businesses and entrepreneurs from the bottom 40 (B40) (Augustin, 2021 and BNM, 2022).

Higher competition in the banking system is preferable to introducing new government schemes. In fact, more centralized initiatives, because they are not tested in the market, may simply become new labels for old forms of subsidies; at the same time, they may create occasions for corruption, support ill-grounded firms, and establish new forms of cronyism. Opening the market to new private players will instead force them and existing banks to compete through innovation; one way for this competition to happen would be by offering packages specifically designed to support emerging entrepreneurs. Furthermore, private credit institutions would be more efficient in evaluating the performance of new businesses.

A mixed scheme that combines a subsidy element with market-based arrangements for credit allocation, which is specifically designed to improve access to finance for SMEs, is a public credit guarantee scheme (CGS). These schemes provide third-party credit risk mitigation to lenders; in return for a fee, the government would absorb a portion of the losses on loans made to SMEs in case of default. Their mixed nature allows less room for distortions in credit markets, unlike more direct forms of intervention, such as state-owned banks (Calice, 2015). With the right fee mechanism, governments would be able to limit their financial disbursement by covering the losses from some loans with the revenues from successful ones.

General Conclusions

THIS PAPER HAS CLEARLY magnified the harsh reality that the urban poor face by presenting the official data. Yet many still fall through the cracks due to statistical issues that contribute to people being excluded from receiving aid. Moreover, many households that earn incomes above the Poverty Line still do not have decent access to basic amenities, healthcare, and education due to the higher cost of living in urban areas.

This calls for a clear paradigm shift: moving away from the obsession of eradicating poverty; departing from unrealistic zero poverty goals; abandoning statistical reports and official presentations that are whitewashed with colourful graphs depicting a deluded sense of pride in poverty eradication.

To do this, we must be objective and sensible in our measurement of poverty, with accurate poverty-line incomes that reflect the realistic current cost of living. Second, we need to identify the best approaches to target vulnerable urban poor groups who fall through the cracks – including non-Malaysian citizens. Third, the recent health and economic crises are an opportunity for us to revise and reform our social protection schemes by seeking the right mechanisms towards enhancing social insurance coverage and implementing active labour market polices. Underlying all these reforms, we must change our perspective toward upholding social mobility. We need a strong and bold drive toward empowering the urban poor to graduate and escape from the generational poverty trap, instead of becoming long-term aid dependents.

The approach we have embraced in the current work is to move away from the idea the urban poor with the resources they do not have, reforms that can place them in the conditions the resources they believe they need. Our motto is: social mobility through entrepreneurship. While entrepreneurship is recognized as an important driver for social mobility, it does not fall off a tree.

Hosts of opportunities are waiting to be discovered. How do they enter in the consciousness of decision-makers? It is here that the fertility of freedom becomes relevant. A free society permits profit-seeking business people to discover unexploited opportunities. The opportunities are socially important but will not be discovered unless private individuals are stimulated to notice them through the lure of entrepreneurial profit (Kirzner, 1982, p. 309).

We believe that the more general reforms that are necessary to spur entrepreneurship among the urban poor are at the educational and institutional levels. In particular, the pillars we see as fundamental for a historical change are:

- Enhancing the protection of property rights and respect of the rule of law by:
  - Fighting corruption;
  - Improving political stability;

- Designing a bigger role for humanist disciplines within the pre-university education path.

By spurring entrepreneurship, we believe these measures will help the system move toward a different growth model centred on savings and investments, rather than on consumption and government spending.

There are other measures that we consider as playing a role in this paradigm shift, and they touch many aspects of the economy. They are:

- *Housing policy reform*: rather than providing homes to the poor, the government should focus on rent support schemes for moving the poor away from "ghettos" to areas where better job opportunities are available;

- *Tax reform*: a modified GST should be reinstated, paired with an income tax reduction; a capital gains tax should be introduced; percentage tax designation institutions should be designed to support bottom-up welfare initiatives;

- *Liberalization of the labour market*: a wider ASEAN job market would support Malaysian talents, offering better opportunities internationally and stimulating competition domestically;

- *Improved access to credit*: microbusinesses should be supported to emerge from the shadow economy; furthermore, higher competition should enter the credit market, together with government guarantee schemes that are supported by fees.

References

APPGM-SDG Secretariat & Malaysian CSO-SDG Alliance (2021), *Submission To Malaysia's 2nd Voluntary National Review On The Sustainable Development Goals 2021*, Putrajaya, Economic Planning Unit.

Augustin, R. (2021), *Digital banking licences a gamechanger for micro SMEs*, «Free Malaysia Today», 16 December, https://www.freemalaysiatoday.com/category/nation/2021/12/16/digital-banking-licenses-a-gamechanger-for-micro-smes/.

Banerjee, A., Breza, E., Duflo, E. and Kinnan, C. (2020), *How microfinance can help entrepreneurs escape the poverty trap*, «Vox EU», 30 March, https://voxeu.org/article/how-microfinance-can-help-entrepreneurs-escape-poverty-trap.

BNM (2016), *Capability and Inclusion Survey 2015*, Kuala Lumpur, Bank Negara Malaysia.

BNM (2017), *Overview of Financial Inclusion in Malaysia*, Kuala Lumpur, Bank Negara Malaysia.

BNM (2018), *The Living Wage: Beyond Making Ends Meet*, Kuala Lumpur, Bank Negara Malaysia.

BNM (2020), *A Vision for Social Protection in Malaysia*, Kuala Lumpur, Bank Negara Malaysia.

BNM (2022), *Five successful applicants for the digital bank licences*, Media Statement, 29 April, Kuala Lumpur, Bank Negara Malaysia.

Bernama (2021), *Amanah Ikhtiar Malaysia denies speculation that it will be privatised*, «Malaymail», Mar 2.

Bertaud, A. and Malpezzi, S. (2001), *Measuring the Costs and Benefits of Urban Land Use Regulation: A Simple Model with an Application to Malaysia*, «Journal of Housing Economics», 10, pp. 393-418.

Boehm-Bawerk, E. von (1884), *The Positive Theory of Capital*, New York, G.E. Stechert & Co., 1930.

Boettke, P.J. and Candela, R.A. (2017), *The Liberty of Progress: Increasing Returns, Institutions, and Entrepreneurship*, «Social Philosophy and Policy», 34, 2, pp. 136-163.

Boettke, P.J. and Coyne, C.J. (2009), *Context Matters: Institutions and Entrepreneurship*, «Foundations and Trends in Entrepreneurship», 5, 3, pp. 135-209.

Burns, S. and Fuller C.S. (2020), *Institutions and Entrepreneurship: Pushing the Boundaries*, «The Quarterly Journal of Austrian Economics», 23, 3-4, pp. 568-612.

Calice, P. (2015), *How can we improve access to credit for SMEs?*, «World Economic Forum», 17 August, https://www.weforum.org/agenda/2015/08/how-can-we-improve-access-to-credit-for-smes/.

DOSM (2019), *Household Income & Basic Amenities Survey Report 2019*, Putrajaya, Department of Statistics Malaysia.

DOSM (2021a), *Household Income Estimates and Incidence of Poverty 2020*, Putrajaya, Department of Statistics Malaysia.

DOSM (2021b), *Labour Force Survey Report 2020*, Putrajaya, Department of Statistics Malaysia.

DOSM (2021c), *Salaries & Wages Survey Report*, Putrajaya, Department of Statistics Malaysia.

DOSM (2022), *Malaysian Economic Statistics Review Vol. 3 2022*, Putrajaya, Department of Statistics Malaysia.

EPU (2004), *Malaysia: 30 Years of Poverty Reduction, Growth and Racial Harmony*, Putrajaya, Prime Minister's Department, Economic Planning Unit.

EPU (2020), *Malaysia Success Story In Poverty Eradication*, Putrajaya, Prime Minister's Department, Economic Planning Unit.

EPU (2021), *Malaysia Voluntary National Review (VNR) 2021*, Putrajaya, Prime Minister's Department, Economic Planning Unit.

Ferlito, C. (2013), *Phoenix Economics. From Crisis to Renascence*, New York, Nova Publishers.

Ferlito, C. (2018), *Affordable Housing and Cyclical Fluctuations: The Malaysian Property Market*, Policy ideas, 51, Kuala Lumpur, Institute for Democracy and Economic Affairs.

Ferlito, C. (2019), *Malaysian Property Market: Affordability and National Housing Policy*, Policy ideas, 61, Kuala Lumpur, Institute for Democracy and Economic Affairs.

Ferlito, C. (2020), *The Entrepreneur: "One, No One and One Hundred Thousand"*, cme EduPaper, 2, Subang Jaya, Center for Market Education.

Garrison, R.W. (1996), *The Flat Tax: Simplicity Desimplified*, «The Free Man», 46, 10, pp. 670-674.

Garrison, R.W. (2001), *Time and Money. The macroeconomics of capital structure*, London and New York, Routledge.

Gjerstad, S.D. and Smith, V. (2014), *Rethinking Housing Bubbles. The Role of Household and Bank Balance Sheets in Modeling Economic Cycles*, New York, Cambridge University Press.

Hannah, L.M., Bertaud, A., Malpezzi, S.J. and Mayo S.K. (1989), *Malaysia – The Housing Sector: Getting the Incentives Right*, World Bank Report No. 7292-MA.

Hanusch, H. and Wackermann, F. (2011), *Can a progressive capital gains tax help avoid the next crisis? Public sector governance in a comprehensive neo-Schumpeterian system*, in S. Kates (ed.), *The Global Financial Crisis: What Have We Learnt?*, Cheltenham and Northampton, Edward Elgar, pp. 57-74.

Hasan, N., Singh, A.K., Agarwal, M.K. and Kushwaha, B.P. (2022), *Evaluating the role of microfinance institutions in enhancing the livelihood of urban poor*, «Journal of Economic and Administrative Sciences», https://doi.org/10.1108/JEAS-09-2021-0175.

Hayek, F.A. von (1931), *Prices and Production*, New York, Augustus M. Kelly, 1967.

Hayek, F.A. von (1937), *Economics and Knowledge*, in *Individualism and Economic Order*, Chicago, University of Chicago Press, 1948, pp. 33-56.

Hayek, F.A. von (1945), *The Use of Knowledge in Society*, «The American Economic Review», XXXV, 4, pp. 519-530.

Huerta de Soto, J. (1992), *Socialism, Economic Calculation and Entrepreneurship*, Cheltenham and Northampton, Edward Elgar, 2010.

Huerta de Soto, J. (2000), *The Austrian School. Market Order and Entrepreneurial Creativity*, Cheltenham and Northampton, Edward Elgar, 2008.

Idris, M.B., Bakar, M.S., Baharuddin, Y. and Syukran, A, (2021), *The Role of Microfinance in Helping the Poor: Amanah Ikhtiar Malaysia as a Model*, «Dirasat: Human and Social Sciences», 48, pp. 673-683.

ILO (2020), *ILO Monitor: COVID-19 and the world of work*, Geneva, International Labour Organization.

Jacobs, J. (1961), *The Death and Life of Great American Cities*, New York, Vintage Books.

Kaur, M. and Amrie, H. (2021), *More poor people in cities than rural areas, says Tok Pa*, «Free Malaysia Today», 15 November, https://www.freemalaysiatoday.com/category/nation/2021/11/15/more-poor-people-in-cities-than-rural-areas-says-tok-pa/.

Kirzner, I.M. (1973), *Competition and entrepreneurship*, Chicago, University of Chicago Press.

Kirzner, I.M. (1982), *The Theory of Entrepreneurship in Economic Growth*, in *The Collected Works of Israel M. Kirzner*, Volume 7: *The Essence of Entrepreneurship and the Nature and Significance of Market Process*, edited by P.J. Boettke and F. Sautet, Carmel, Liberty Fund, 2018, pp. 305-309.

KRI (2018), *State of Households 2018: Different Realities*, Kuala Lumpur, Khazanah Research Institute.

KRI (2021), *Building Resilience Towards Inclusive Social Protection In Malaysia*, Kuala Lumpur, Khazanah Research Institute.

Lachmann, L.M. (1973), *Macro-economic Thinking and the Market Economy. An essay on the neglect of the micro-foundations and its consequences*, London, The Institute of Economic Affairs.

Lavoie, D. (1985a), *Rivalry and Central Planning. The socialist calculation debate reconsidered*, Cambridge, Cambridge University Press.

Lavoie, D. (1985b), *National Economic Planning: What Is Left?*, Cambridge, Ballinger Publishing.

Lee, N. and Rodríguez-Pose, A. (2021), *Entrepreneurship and the fight against poverty in US cities*, «Economy and Space», 53, 1, pp. 31-52.

Levy-Carciente, S. and Montanari, L. (2021), *International Property Rights Index 2021*, Washington, DC, Property Rights Alliance.

Lim, L.L. (2021), *The socioeconomic impacts of COVID-19 in Malaysia: Policy review and guidance for protecting the most vulnerable and supporting enterprises*, «International Labour Organization».

Lim, T.G., Chander, R. and Hunter, M. (2021), *My Say: Reset the 12MP's approach to poverty*, «The Edge Markets», 26 October, https://www.theedgemarkets.com/article/my-say-reset-12mps-approach-poverty.

Malpezzi, S. (2014), *Global Perspectives on Housing Markets and Policy*, Working Paper #3, New York, Marron Institute of Urban Management, New York University.

Malpezzi, S. and Wachter, S.M. (2005), *The Role of Speculation in Real Estate Cycles*, «Journal of Real Estate Literature», 13, 2, pp. 143-164.

McCloskey, D.N. (2016), *The Great Enrichment: A Humanistic and Social Scientific Account*, «Social Science History», 40, 4, pp. 583-598, DOI: https://doi.org/10.1017/ssh.2016.23.

Minsky, H.P. (1982), *Can "It" Happen Again? Essays on Instability and Finance*, London and New York, Routledge, 2016.

Minsky, H.P. (2008), *Stabilizing an Unstable Economy*, New York, McGraw-Hill.

Mises, L. von (1920), *Economic Calculation in the Socialist Commonwealth*, in *Collectivist Economic Planning*, edited by F.A. von Hayek, London, Routledge & Kegan Paul, 1935, pp. 87-130.

Morris, M. (2022), *Entrepreneurship and the Poverty Experience*, «Oxford Research Encyclopedia of Business and Management», DOI: https://doi.org/10.1093/acrefore/9780190224851.013.357.

Omar, M.A. and Inaba, K. (2020), *Does financial inclusion reduce poverty and income inequality in developing countries? A panel data analysis*, «Journal of *Economic Structures*», 9, 37, pp. 1-25, DOI: https://doi.org/10.1186/s40008-020-00214-4.

Ong, J. (2020), *Education Ministry: Over one in three students couldn't access online learning during MCO*, «Malaymail», Jul 6.

Park, C.Y. (2018), *How Financial Inclusion Reduces Poverty, Income Inequality,* «Asian Development Blog», Apr 3, https://blogs.adb.org/blog/how-financial-inclusion-reduces-poverty-income-inequality.

Phaneuf, E. (2020), *The Problems of Knowledge and Economic Calculation*, EduPaper Nr 4, Subang Jaya, Center for Market Education.

Prychitko, D.L. (2010), *Competing Explanations of the Minsky Moment: The Financial Instability Hypothesis in Light of Austrian Theory*, «The Review of Austrian Economics», 23, pp. 199-221.

Ravallion, M. (1998), *Poverty lines in theory and practice*, «LMS Working Paper», 133, The World Bank.

Saad, N. M. (2012), *Microfinance and Prospect for Islamic Microfinance Products: The Case of Amanah Ikhtiar Malaysia*. «Advances in Social Science», 1, 1.

Salgotra, A.K., Kandari, P. and Bahuguna, U. (2021), *Does Access to Finance Eradicate Poverty? A Case Study of Mudra Beneficiaries,* «Journal of Asian Finance, Economics and Business», 8, 1, pp. 637-646, DOI: https://doi.org/10.13106/jafeb.2021.vol8.no1.637.

Satar, N. and Kassim, S. (2020), *Issues and Challenges in Financing the Poor: Lessons Learned from Islamic Microfinance Institutions*. «European Journal of Islamic Finance», 15, DOI:https://doi.org/10.13135/2421-2172/2832.

Schumpeter, J.A. (1911), *The theory of economic development: An inquiry into profits, capital, credit, interest, and the business cycle*, New Brunswick and London, Transaction Publishers, 1983.

Schumpeter, J.A. (1918), *The Crisis of the Tax State*, in *The Economics and Sociology of Capitalism*, Princeton, NJ, Princeton University Press, 1991, pp. 99-140.

Silvestri, P. (2019), *Explaining Percentage Tax Designation Institutions. Restarting from Sugden's Contractarianism*, paper presented at the HEIRS Conference 2019 held in Rome, Italy.

Singh, V. (2021), *Developing a Modern Tax Framework for Malaysia*, cme Policy Brief, 2, Subang Jaya, Center for Market Education.

Stier, A., Berman, M. and Bettencourt, L. (2020), *COVID-19 attack rate increases with city size*", «arXiv preprint», https://arxiv.org/abs/2003.10376.

The Edge Markets. (2021*), Cover Story: Withdrawal of Account 1 shook EPF to its core, says Amir,* «The Edge Markets», June 24, https://www.theedgemarkets.com/article/cover-story-withdrawal-account-1-shook-epf-its-core-says-amir.

The Star (2019), *Poorer than we think: Malaysia's official poverty figures 'vastly' undercounted, says UN expert,* «The Star», 23 August, https://www.thestar.com.my/news/nation/2019/08/23/poorer-than-we-think-malaysias-official-poverty-figures-vastly-undercounted-says-un-expert.

UNICEF (2018), *Children Without*, Putrajaya, UNICEF Malaysia.

UNICEF (2020), *Families on the Edge Issue 1*, Putrajaya, UNICEF Malaysia.

UNICEF (2021), *Families on the Edge Issue 4*, Putrajaya, UNICEF Malaysia.

UNHCR (2022), *Figures at a Glance in Malaysia*, https://www.unhcr.org/en-my/figures-at-a-glance-in-malaysia.html.

Weerasena, B. and Lim, B. (2022), *Repeated EPF withdrawals a ticking time bomb*, «Malay Mail», 17 March, https://www.malaymail.com/news/what-you-think/2022/03/17/repeated-epf-withdrawals-a-ticking-time-bomb-benedict-weerasena-and-abel-be/2047893.

Wahab, F. (2022), *KL's hardcore poor shot up by 270% after pandemic,* «The Star», 4 April, https://www.thestar.com.my/metro/metro-news/2022/04/04/kls-hardcore-poor-shot-up-by-270-after-pandemic

World Bank (2020), *A Silver Lining: Productive and Inclusive Aging for Malaysia*, https://www.worldbank.org/en/country/malaysia/publication/a-silver-lining-productive-and-inclusive-aging-for-malaysia.

World Economic Forum (2018), *Global Competitiveness Index: Ease of access to loans, 1-7 (best)*, «World Bank TCdata 360», https://tcdata360.worldbank.org/indicators/inv.acc.loan?country=MYS&indicator=527&countries=THA,IDN,SGP&viz=line_chart&years=2007,2017&indicators=944&compareBy=region.

Zain, R.M. (2007), *Understanding the formulation of the revised poverty line in Malaysia*, «Akademika», 70, 1, pp. 21-39.